Hiking the Green Mountains

Hiking the Green Mountains

A Guide to 40 of the Region's Best Hiking Adventures

Second Edition

Lisa Ballard and Mark Aiken

FALCONGUIDES

GUILFORD, CONNECTICUT

FALCONGUIDES®

An imprint of Globe Pequot, the trade division of
The Rowman & Littlefield Publishing Group, Inc.
4501 Forbes Blvd., Ste. 200
Lanham, MD 20706
www.rowman.com
Falcon and FalconGuides are registered trademarks and Make Adventure Your Story is a trademark
of The Rowman & Littlefield Publishing Group, Inc.

Distributed by NATIONAL BOOK NETWORK

British Library Cataloguing-in-Publication Information available

Library of Congress Cataloging-in-Publication Data

Names: Ballard, Lisa Densmore, author.
Title: Hiking the Green Mountains : a guide to 40 of the region's best hiking adventures / Lisa
    Densmore Ballard and Mark Aiken.
Description: 2nd Edition. | Guilford, Connecticut : FalconGuides, [2022] | "A previous edition of this
    book was published by Falcon Publishing, Inc., in 2009"–T.p. verso. | Includes bibliographical
    references and index. | Summary: "Features concise descriptions and detailed maps for 40 easy-
    to-follow trails that allow hikers of all levels to enjoy beautiful views, get fit in the outdoors, and
    learn about the region's history" — Provided by publisher.
Identifiers: LCCN 2021040540 (print) | LCCN 2021040541 (ebook) | ISBN 9781493043309
    (Trade Paperback : acid-free paper) | ISBN 9781493043316 (ePub)
Subjects: LCSH: Hiking—Vermont—Green Mountains—Guidebooks. | Day hiking—Vermont—Green
    Mountains—Guidebooks. | Walking—Vermont—Green Mountains—Guidebooks. | Backpacking—
    Vermont—Green Mountains—Guidebooks. | Trails—Vermont—Green Mountains—Guidebooks. |
    Outdoor recreation—Vermont—Green Mountains—Guidebooks. | Green Mountains (Vt.) —
    Description and travel. | Green Mountains (Vt.) —Guidebooks.
Classification: LCC GV199.42.V42 G743 2022 (print) | LCC GV199.42.V42
    (ebook) | DDC 796.5109743—dc23
LC record available at https://lccn.loc.gov/2021040540
LC ebook record available at https://lccn.loc.gov/2021040541

∞™ The paper used in this publication meets the minimum requirements of American National Standard
for Information Sciences—Permanence of Paper for Printed Library Materials, ANSI/NISO Z39.48-1992.

Contents

North-Central Green Mountains: Brandon Gap to Huntington

Waterbury-Stowe Area: Waterbury to Jeffersonville

Northern Green Mountains: Johnson to the Canadian Border

Kilometers

Miles

N

QUEBEC

CANADA
USA

Alburg
Swanton
Enosburg Falls
Richford
North Troy
Newport
Derby Line
Derby Center

Lake
Champlain
Saint Albans
Orleans
Barton
Albany
West Burke

Milton
Jeffersonville
Johnson
Hyde Park
Lyndonville

Essex
Junction
Morrisville

Burlington
Stowe
Cabot

South
Burlington
Waterbury
Marshfield
Montpelier
Barre
Wells River
Newbury
Bradford

Vergennes
Bristol
Northfield
VERMONT

NEW
HAMPSHIRE

GREEN
MOUNTAIN
NATIONAL
FOREST

Woodstock
Rutland
Poultney
Ludlow
Perkinsville

NEW
YORK

Manchester
Bellows Falls
North Westminster
Westminster
Saxtons River

GREEN
MOUNTAIN
NATIONAL
FOREST
Newfane

North Bennington
Old
Bennington
Jacksonville

MASSACHUSETTS

To Alison, my hiking partner
(Mark Aiken)

To my son, Parker Densmore, my favorite hiking buddy
(Lisa Ballard)

Acknowledgments

Lisa's Acknowledgements

While this book bears my name and Mark Aiken's name, many have contributed to its pages in ways for which I am grateful. First, I would like to thank Mark for re-hiking the routes (and adding some new ones) and making the updates for this second edition. He literally did the legwork this time.

This book could not exist without help from the Green Mountain Club; the USDA Green Mountain National Forest; the Vermont Department of Forests, Parks and Recreation; the Vermont Youth Conservation Corps; and the Westmore Association Trails Committee. Thank you to the many people in these groups who maintain the trails and campsites that allow the rest of us to enjoy these beautiful mountains and who provided invaluable insights when I wrote the first edition.

I'm also grateful to Peter Sachs at Lowa, my longtime hiking boot sponsor. With his generous supply of footwear, my feet are always happy wherever I trek, including the older, oft eroded and wet routes in the Green Mountains. And finally, a sincere thanks to the many people who accompanied me when I hiked the trails that are the basis for this book. I appreciated your patience while I took field notes, your willingness to be in my photos, and, most of all, your companionship on the trail.

Mark's Acknowledgments

I will be forever grateful to Lisa Ballard for her masterful first edition of this book. A lot happened in twelve years, but it did not feel like work to hike these routes, noting changes and adding new ones. Lisa, your writing and photography skills, your passion, and your knowledge are inspirational.

I appreciate Matt Krebs, operations manager of the Green Mountain Club, for his incredible patience, expertise, and knowledge in answering a zillion questions. And then he answered a zillion-and-one follow-up questions. I further appreciate the Green Mountain Club, their paid staff, and their volunteers for stewarding and maintaining over 400 miles of trails in Vermont—each mile of which greatly improves the quality of life in this beautiful state.

I appreciate the many staffers from the Vermont Department of Forests, Parks and Recreation who either answered my questions or found someone who could. Thank you to Jessica Savage, recreation manager at VFPR, and the many trail workers who keep up trails on state land.

Scott Wixsom, Danna Strout, and Cera Hurley of the Green Mountain National Forest patiently answered question after question. I appreciate Doug McKain and Ruth Penfield for their vast knowledge of the trails in central Vermont that they steward—and of seemingly every inch of trail from Massachusetts to Canada. Thanks to my running, hiking, and biking partners Alex and Kevin McAleer for the beta on the trails in your area. Many volunteers from the Bennington section of the Long Trail chimed in to answer questions.

Thanks to Sue Hoxie of the Moosalamoo Association for finding the people with the answers about her area. Also to Daniel Ian Smith and Irene Salerno of the Westmore Association for answering my questions about northern Vermont hikes. Vermont Youth Conservation Corps and North Woods Stewardship Center crews are the future—thank you for your work on trails all over Vermont.

Thank you to Lucie Keene, Neil Preston, Liz Yasewicz, Gunnar Aiken, and Ingrid Aiken for hiking with me and putting up with my note-taking, photo-shooting, and GPS-fiddling on the trail. I want to recognize trail volunteers—and donors who support trails—everywhere. Good trails do not just happen in the twenty-first century; they need protection, maintenance, and stewardship . . . or, simply, they will disappear. Thanks to everyone—anyone—who values trails of all kinds.

Katie O'Dell, my editor at Globe Pequot, is simply awesome. Thank you.

Finally, my wife, Alison, accompanied me on many of the hikes (often with our kids), and just as often she stayed home (with the kids). Without her, this second edition—or any of my writing projects—would simply never happen.

Meet Your Guides

Born and raised in Vermont, **Mark Aiken** has spent a lifetime exploring the Green Mountains—except for the decade he spent in the Southwest ski instructing and whitewater and backcountry guiding.

Returning to Vermont, he continued his Green Mountain explorations as a backcountry skier, as a trail runner (which enabled him to cover more ground quickly), and as a husband and dad. "I cover slightly less ground and more slowly with the kids, but I get a completely different perspective and experience," he says, noting that his eight-year-old and six-year-old are not just avid hikers—they are ardent trail-builders.

An award-winning freelance writer, Mark is a professional ski instructor who contributes regularly to *32 Degrees*, the

MARK AIKEN

national magazine of Professional Ski Instructors of America. He also covers Vermont topics in regional magazines like *Vermont Magazine*, *Stowe Guide & Magazine*, *Woodstock*, *Upper Valley Image*, and *Best of Burlington*. He has also published in national publications including *SKI*, *Backpacker*, *Trail Runner*, and the *New York Times*.

When he isn't at his writing desk, he can be found on the slopes or the trails . . . or feeding his chickens at his home in Vermont.

Lisa Ballard (formerly Lisa Densmore) has been hiking in the Green Mountains for over forty-five years. A resident of the state off and on, she went to high school at Stratton Mountain School and then later moved back to Stratton Mountain while competing on the Women's Pro Ski Tour. She then spent two decades living in Hanover, New Hampshire, on the Vermont–New Hampshire border, within two hours of most trailheads in Vermont.

A professional freelance journalist since 1991, Lisa has garnered three Emmys (and five additional nominations) for her work in outdoor television. The Outdoor Writers Association of America, the North American Snowsports Journalists Association, and the Society of American Travel Writers have each bestowed numerous awards on Lisa for her work, not only in television, but also as a writer and photographer, which is her main gig nowadays. You can find samples of her work on her website, LisaBallardOutdoors.com.

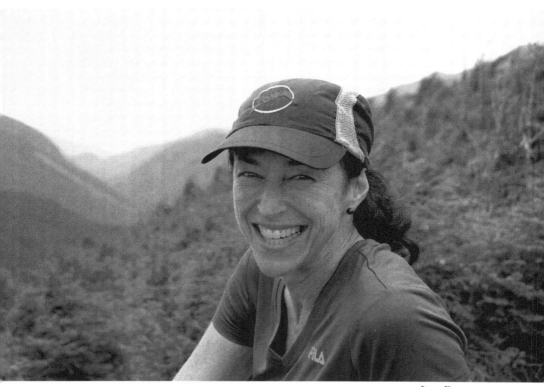

LISA BALLARD

Though Lisa now splits her time between homes in Montana and the Adirondacks, you can read her stories, often about hiking in Vermont and other parts of the world, in local magazines including *Upper Valley Image* and *Woodstock Magazine*. Lisa is the author of thirteen books including *Hiking the Adirondacks*, *Best Easy Day Hikes Adirondacks*, and *Hiking the White Mountains* from FalconGuides.

Introduction

Geology of the Green Mountains

The Green Mountains of Vermont are composed mainly of igneous granite and quartz, as well as metamorphic phyllite, schist, quartzite, greenstone, slate, and gneiss. The origin of the name "Green Mountains" is unclear, but one theory is because of the predominance of green-colored rock. The other theory is that the mountains are forested up to higher elevations than the neighboring Adirondacks to the west in New York and the White Mountains to the east in New Hampshire. About three-quarters of Vermont remains forested.

The basic topography was formed about 12,000 years ago when the last ice age receded. As the mile-deep ice retreated, it gouged the softer rock, creating the ledges and cliffs that provide many of the best hiking destinations today. A classic example is the sheer cliffs of Mount Pisgah over Lake Willoughby (see hike 37). The glaciers deposited large boulders, called *glacial erratics,* throughout the backcountry. They also left behind the scree and rocks that tumble down various Vermont hillsides, such as the boulder pile at White Rocks Ice Beds (see hike 11).

Flora

With their relatively low base elevations and exposed summits, the tallest peaks in the Green Mountains boast four different climate zones, each with distinct flora. Trailheads are typically below 2,000 feet in the zone called the eastern deciduous forest, made up primarily of sugar maple, beech, poplar, and yellow birch, or the mixed northern forest, which adds evergreens into the mix.

Wildflowers are plentiful from early spring through early fall. In the spring look for blooming trillium, bunchberry, and trout lily along the forest floor. During summer devil's paintbrush, violets, and various wild orchids give color to the woods and clearings. Early autumn's goldenrod, black-eyed Susans, and asters add to the vibrant fall foliage. Interestingly, the autumnal explosion of reds, oranges, and yellows is not due to an endemic strain of maple, but rather to the soil and climate. Red clover, Vermont's state flower, blooms from May through October. You'll also find a number of mushroom species growing on the forest floor and on tree trunks.

Vermont's state flower is the red clover.
Lisa Ballard

1

Entering the alpine zone at the edge of the krummholz on Camel's Hump. LISA BALLARD

At 2,600 feet, trails begin to enter the boreal forest, which is mainly coniferous balsam fir, spruce, cedar, and hemlock. Species such as mountain ash and white (paper) birch also grow in the boreal zone. Flora in this zone can handle more extreme winter climates and are more exposed to biting wind, hoar frost, and fog.

Above 3,500 feet, trails pass through a subalpine zone called krummholz, which is composed of severely stunted, unevenly shaped trees that tend to grow with their "backs to the wind and their heads in the snow." With the extremely short growing season and severe weather conditions, many of these thigh-high shrubs are actually hundreds of years old. Wild blueberry, rhodera, and Labrador tea are also common in the subalpine zone.

Five of the peaks in the Green Mountains—Mount Mansfield, Mount Abraham, Lincoln Peak, Killington Peak, and Camel's Hump—have elevations over 4,000 feet. Three of these summits have a fragile alpine zone, which primarily supports low ground covers and lichens. Most alpine plants here are similar to those found thousands of miles to the north in the Arctic Circle, though they are genetically isolated and considered rare or endangered. The grasses that grow among the rocks in the alpine zone are actually rare sedges. In June and July, mountain sandwort, diapensia, and other delicate flowers add color and interest above tree line.

Fauna

Vermont has 42 species of reptiles and amphibians, 58 mammals, and 235 birds. Many are visible from the hiking trails if you are lucky. More likely, you will see animal tracks and scat. Whitetail deer and moose are the only wild ungulates in the state. Snowshoe hares, beavers, porcupines, red and gray squirrels, chipmunks, skunks, and raccoons are among the more common small mammals. You can hike in the Green Mountains for a lifetime and never see a bobcat, fisher, coyote, or fox, but they are in the woods as well.

Common birds along the trail include robins, tree swallows, black-capped chickadees, red-winged blackbirds, various woodpeckers, blue jays, ruffed grouse, and peregrine falcons. The Forest Service will close cliff areas to hikers if peregrines decide to nest there, so it is worth checking if you are planning a hike to a cliff-top destination from early May through mid-August.

A red squirrel packs up for winter on Bluff Mountain. MARK AIKEN

The most dangerous creature in Vermont's backcountry is the black bear. In general, a bear will avoid hikers, but a hungry bear will raid a campsite if it smells food, and the bear's sense of smell is very keen. It will also defend a natural food source and its cubs. To minimize the chance of a bear encounter, do the following:

- Hike in a group during daylight hours.
- Make noise by talking or singing as you walk.
- Leave hair spray, cologne, scented soaps, and hand lotions at home.
- Never eat food or feed a dog in your tent.
- Do not clean dishes within 100 feet of your campsite.

Always hang food, trash, and other scented items in a designated bear bag or bear-proof canister away from your shelter or campsite. The bag should be at least 12 feet off the ground and at least 8 feet away from the trunk of the tree.

Forests and Parks

Many of the trails in this book are located within the USDA Green Mountain National Forest. This 400,000-acre forest extends from the southern border of the state along the Green Mountains to Route 103, then from north of US 4 to just south of Waitsfield. Other trails, such as the Healdville Trail on Okemo Mountain (see hike 8), are located in state forests. Some of the trailheads, such as the start of the Sunset Ridge Trail on Mount Mansfield (see hike 31), are in state parks but the routes cross into state or national forest above the trailhead. Although the Appalachian Trail corridor is technically national park, none of the trails in this book traverse land that is managed as a national park. Two of the hikes, the White Rocks Cliffs and the White Rocks Ice Beds (see hikes 10 and 11), are in a designated National Scenic Area. These distinctions do not affect hikers, unless you have a dog. Leash laws vary depending on who manages the land.

Every hike listed is stewarded by an organization and is available for use by the public. Hikers should always treat open spaces respectfully. Specific private landowner conditions, if any, are noted.

Long Trail and Appalachian Trail

In 1910 the Green Mountain Club (GMC) established the Long Trail (LT), the first long-distance hiking trail in the United States. It was completed in 1930 and travels 272 miles along the high spine of the Green Mountains from the Massachusetts border to the Canadian border.

Each year many "through-hikers" attempt to traverse the entire LT, though those in the southern half of Vermont might be attempting the 2,174-mile Appalachian National Scenic Trail (AT), which begins in Georgia and ends in Maine. The two trails coincide for about 100 miles in Vermont, from the Massachusetts border to just north of US 4 near Deer Leap Mountain (see hike 14). Both trails are marked with

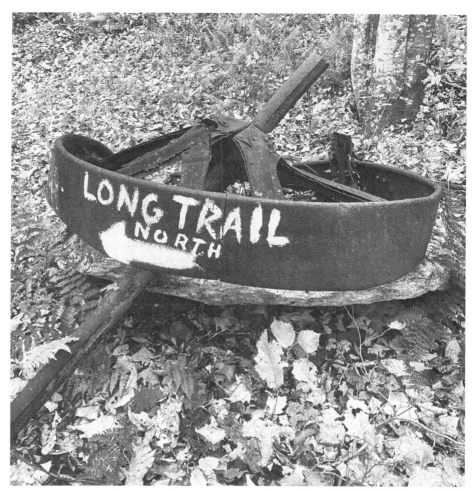

Creative signage on the Long Trail. MARK AIKEN

white blazes (a vertical rectangle painted on sturdy trees or bedrock). Side trails that lead to the AT/LT are marked by blue blazes.

With a paid staff of seasonal and year-round employees plus hundreds of enthusiastic volunteers arranged in sections throughout Vermont, the GMC is the nonprofit steward, maintainer, and advocate for over 400 miles of trails in Vermont.

Backpacking and Camping

The GMC maintains about seventy rustic cabins, shelters, and tent sites along Vermont's hiking trails. They are available on a first-come, first-served basis and typically sleep eight to ten people. If your party does not fill the cabin or shelter, please allow others to share the space with you.

Interior of Pico Shelter on Pico Peak. LISA BALLARD

In addition, the GMC and other trail maintenance groups have a number of tent platforms and primitive campsites scattered throughout the Green Mountains. During the summer and early fall, expect to pay a small nightly fee per person for the use of cabins, shelters, and designated campsites. Most shelters and campsites have a privy (outhouse), a specific place to wash dishes, a fire pit, and a water source. Always filter water or use another water-purification method in the Green Mountains to avoid contracting the giardia parasite or another waterborne illness.

Some of the trailheads in this book are located in state parks with campsites that can accommodate car camping and RVs. Call ahead to be sure there is enough space, particularly during the summer and the fall foliage season (late September through mid-October). State campsites are closed during the winter and early spring.

Camping is also permitted elsewhere on public lands. Select a site that is below tree line and at least 150 feet away from trails and water sources. And try to find a site on a durable surface to minimize impact to the environment. Campfires are not recommended in the Vermont backcountry. Plan to cook over a portable camping stove.

Weather

Vermont has a temperate climate, with warm, humid summers and cold, snowy winters. The northeastern part of the state, called the "Northeast Kingdom," has exceptionally cold winters. The highest recorded temperature in the state was 105 degrees Fahrenheit in 1911. The record low was minus 50 degrees in 1933. The weather tends to present much greater hazards to hikers in the Green Mountains than wildlife.

The chart below gives average temperature by month in the state. Keep in mind that this is at the trailhead. Subtract 3 to 5 degrees for each 1,000 feet of elevation that you climb. For example, if it is 80 degrees at the base of Mount Mansfield, it might be 55 degrees at the summit, not including a stiff windchill.

Heat. July is particularly hot and humid, though June and August can have equally sticky days. Be sure to stay hydrated to avoid heat stroke. Experienced hikers sometimes bring an extra shirt to stay drier.

Vermont: Average Temperature High/Low by Month

Month	Jan	Feb	Mar	Apr	May	Jun	Jul	Aug	Sep	Oct	Nov	Dec
Avg High	27	31	40	55	67	76	81	79	70	57	46	33
Avg Low	10	13	22	35	45	55	60	59	51	39	31	19

Data gathered from National Weather Service records (weather.gov)

Lightning. If you are hiking and hear thunder, assume lightning too. At the slightest hint of a storm, head immediately below tree line to an area where the trees are at least twice as tall as you are. If this is impossible, try to find a low spot on the ridge where you can hunker down. Even below tree line, it is not safe to use a tree for shelter, especially a tall one. Find a depression in the ground and crouch down until the storm passes. If there are other people with you, spread out so that if lightning strikes, it does not hit everyone in your party.

Snow and ice. The average yearly snowfall in Vermont is 50 to 100 inches, but most of that blows off the tops of mountains and other areas of exposed rock. What's more, rock slab tends to freeze up before the rest of the trail. At the first signs of frost, it is

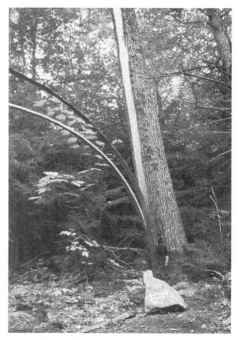

A tree hit by lightning beside the trail.
LISA BALLARD

a good idea to bring traction aids, such as crampons, micro-spikes, and hiking poles, when you venture into the backcountry. Snowshoes are a must if the snow gets deep.

Once in a while, the Green Mountains get hit by ice storms rather than snow. Ice from these storms clings to trees, causing them to bend radically and sometimes break from the weight. Major ice storms can render hiking routes impassable due to tree damage. The same is true when a microburst hits. Though both of these types of storms are rare, they do happen. It can take trail crews many weeks to reopen a route due to the extensive damage done by these two natural phenomena. More common are what locals refer to as "thaw-freeze" cycles—warm snow-and-ice-melting temperatures followed by a sharp temperature drop causing dangerously slick conditions. Crampons and micro-spikes become necessary equipment in such conditions—as well as the prudence to turn around if you don't have this equipment in your kit.

Be Prepared: Backcountry Safety and Hazards

While the Green Mountains are relatively low compared to places like the Rockies or the Sierra Nevada, they are still mountains. As such, bad weather is foremost among the risks associated with hiking and backpacking here. The old saying "If you don't like the weather, wait a few moments" is often true. Regardless of the time of year, always bring layers of clothing, including a fleece or wool mid-layer for warmth and a waterproof, breathable jacket to block wind and precipitation.

Mud. Many trails are closed during the notorious Vermont mud season, which begins with snowmelt and ends by late May. But Vermont still averages 4 inches of rain per month in the summer, so mud is common on the trails here. Perennially muddy areas usually have narrow puncheon (split log) walkways across them to help keep your feet dry. Otherwise, you will have to depend on your rock-hopping skills. Avoid walking off the trail to miss a mud puddle, which only widens the trail over time, contributes to erosion, and eventually leads to a costly trail relocation.

A typical muddy trail during mud season or after a rainstorm LISA BALLARD

◀ *Hiker on the Long Trail to Sterling Pond in March.* LISA BALLARD

Brooks and streams. Streams are fickle in the Green Mountains. They might be swollen and impassable during spring runoff or after a heavy rainstorm, and they might dry up completely by mid-August. Hiking poles can help you maintain your balance during a tricky stream crossing.

Bugs. Unfortunately, the Green Mountains are home to blackflies, mosquitoes, and other pesky insects.. Deer ticks that carry Lyme and other diseases have become increasingly prevalent. Thorough tick checks are highly recommended after every outing. Bug spray is often a must during the spring and the summer months on the hiking trail. Wearing a ball cap or a wide-brimmed hat also helps.

Poison plants. There are only two poison plants in Vermont: poison sumac and poison ivy. You are unlikely to find poison sumac along a hiking trail because it prefers low-lying wet soil. Poison ivy, however, is common below 2,000 feet. Its usual form is a ground cover or low shrub, but it can also wind its way up tree trunks as a vine. Mature poison ivy vines become woody, resembling their host trees. Poison ivy leaves appear in clusters of three. Young leaves have a shiny olive hue, with hints of red. During the summer the leaves are true green, and in the fall they often turn bright red or red and yellow. Skin contact with any part of the poison ivy plant, dead or alive, will likely result in an itchy red rash. The rash is actually caused by urushiol oil and can appear anywhere from a few hours to several days later. If you suspect that

Poison ivy with its three leaves and red stems. Lisa Ballard

you came in contact with poison ivy, wash the area with soap and water as soon as possible to remove the oil. Depending on how sensitive you are, you have up to two hours to avoid the rash by thoroughly washing the exposed area.

Hiker's Checklist

The following is a basic list of things to put in your pack to ensure you are prepared for a day in the backcountry. This is a fair-weather list. Winter hikers will need additional items such as a down jacket, gaiters, snowshoes, crampons or microspikes, gloves, and goggles. For more information, visit www.greenmountainclub.org/the-long-trail/trip-planning.

- ❑ Bug spray
- ❑ Navigation (map and compass and GPS unit)
- ❑ Sun protection (sunglasses, hat with a brim, sunscreen)
- ❑ Insulation (extra clothing layers, wool hat, rain gear)
- ❑ Illumination (headlamp or flashlight)
- ❑ First-aid kit including any medications you take regularly
- ❑ Fire (waterproof matches or reliable lighter)
- ❑ Tools and repair kit (and the knowledge to use them)
- ❑ Nutrition (extra food)
- ❑ Hydration (extra water or water treatment or filtration system)
- ❑ Emergency shelter (tarp or blanket)
- ❑ Whistle
- ❑ Bandana or other all-purpose rag
- ❑ Camera

Hunting Seasons

There are several hunting seasons in Vermont. The dates change annually, but in general, bear season begins around September 1 and runs through mid-November. Various moose seasons occur throughout October; deer season begins in early November. Most hunters avoid popular hiking corridors, but it is always better to err on the side of safety. If you are planning to hike during hunting season, wear a blaze-orange hat, jacket, and/or vest. Bright red is less effective if the leaves are still on the trees because the leaves are also red, though anything colorful is better than browns and blacks.

Zero Impact

Leave only footprints and take only memories. It is every hiker's responsibility to help keep the backcountry as pristine as possible so that future generations can have the same enjoyable experiences. Here are several additional things that you can do to help:

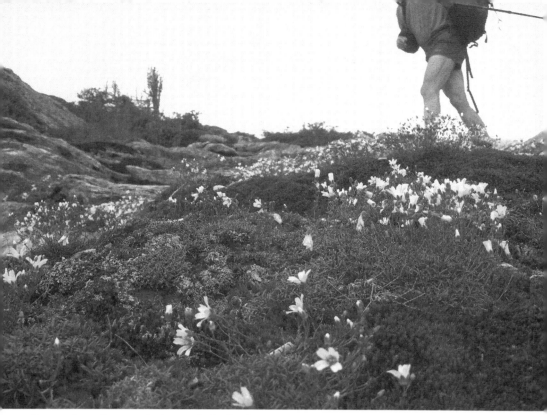

Stay on the trail so you don't trample fragile plants. LISA BALLARD

- Limit the number in your party to eight or fewer.
- Avoid using soaps within 150 yards of water sources.
- Either bury or pack out human and dog waste.
- Carry out what you carry in.
- Leave plants and wildlife alone.

Before You Hit the Trail

The trails in this guidebook were selected primarily because they are all truly interesting, scenic hikes. They are spread geographically from the south end to the north end of the state to allow a number of options regardless of location. In addition, the routes vary by mileage and vertical rise. To find the best route near you, start with the fitness level of the weakest person in your party, then pick a hike length that is half what he or she is comfortable walking on a flat, paved sidewalk. For example, if you feel you can handle 4 miles in town, start with a hike that is 2 miles or less and then build up from there.

For each hike you will find the following information.

Beneath the name of each hike is a brief description of the hike, often listing some of its highlights.

General Location

This is a short summary of the starting location for the hike. There may not be amenities at these locations.

Distance

The distance specified in each description is the total distance for the hike. For example, if it's an out-and-back hike that is 3 miles one way, the distance will be noted as 6 miles.

Hiking mileages—regardless of how painstakingly and with which equipment they are measured—will vary. Matt Krebs, operations manager of the Green Mountain Club, which stewards over 400 miles of trails (including many of the routes described in this book), has this to say about the state-of-the-art equipment that the GMC uses to determine trail mileage: "If two different people go out on the same trail on two different days using the same equipment, they are likely to come back with two different mileage numbers." Hike lengths in this guide have been cross-referenced with available resources, including topographic maps, government measurements, the authors' GPS measurements, trail signs and markers, and other guidebooks. Different resources don't always agree, so the final figure is sometimes the authors' best estimate; your GPS watch may well give you a different number too. Therefore, pay close attention to physical landmarks in addition to mileages in this book and on trail signs.

Regarding trail signs, in this book we have referred whenever possible to natural features and trail intersections (both of which could also change!) instead of signs. Signs aren't permanent.

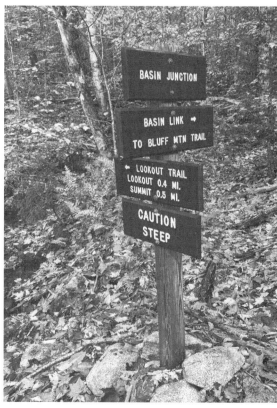

Signs are helpful, but they are not permanent and can't be relied on. MARK AIKEN

Hiking Time

This is a subjective measurement. Very fit, fast-moving hikers will be able to complete a route in less time. Slower-moving hikers or those preoccupied with activities such as photography may take longer. In general, super-fit expert hikers might be able to cover 2 miles per hour if the terrain is relatively smooth and not too steep and if they never stop moving. The average person usually hikes at half that speed, about 1 mile per hour. We used the following formula to estimate hiking time: half the total distance plus one hour for every 1,000 vertical feet. In other words, if a hike is 6 miles long and climbs 2,000 vertical feet, it will take five hours. In the end, hiking times are an educated guess and ultimately depend on how fit you are and how much you dally at each viewpoint.

Highest Point and Elevation Gain

Elevation is often the most important factor in determining a hike's difficulty. The highest point reached on each hike is provided. Elevation gain refers to the change between the hike's lowest point (often, but not always, at the trailhead) and the high point, taking into account all ups and downs.

Absolute elevation also affects difficulty. At high elevations, lower atmospheric pressure creates "thin air" that requires higher breathing rates and more effort to pull enough oxygen into the lungs. None of the hikes in Vermont reach elevations with decreased oxygen levels in the air. But some Vermont peaks can be as rugged, steep, and exposed as mountains anywhere.

Difficulty

Assessing a hike's difficulty is subjective. The maximum elevation, vertical gain, and length of the hike all play a role, as do trail conditions, weather, and the hiker's physical condition. To make ratings as objective as possible, we used the following criteria:

Easy: Under 2 miles round-trip *and* under 500 feet elevation gain.
Moderate: 2 to 5 miles round-trip *or* 500 feet to 1,200 feet elevation gain.
More challenging: More than 5 miles but less than 8 miles round-trip *or* more than 1,200 feet but less than 2,000 feet elevation gain.
Very strenuous: More than 8 miles round-trip *or* 2,000 feet or more elevation gain.

Note that these ratings are a general guideline. In some cases, a hike might be rated higher or lower than these criteria based on terrain. Also, take note: Carrying a heavy backpack can make even an "easy" day hike fairly strenuous.

When to Go

Most hikes in this book are open nearly year-round. The notable exception occurs during Vermont's infamous "fifth season"—that is, mud season. At the end of a long winter, when the snow melts, some Vermont trails become a muddy soup. In these conditions, widespread human use can inflict profound damage. Therefore, many trail managers, including the Vermont Department of Forests, Parks and Recreation and the Green Mountain Club, generally restrict access to trail networks—particularly those trails at higher elevations and above tree line—from the beginning of mud season, which varies depending on the winter but usually starts in late April, until Memorial Day weekend. Check websites or make calls in the spring for the latest information on closures.

Also, take note: Vermont winters are extreme. With over 300 inches of annual snowfall in some areas covered in this book, a hike in February will look much different than the same hike from May until November. Temperatures vary—more now than ever before—and, almost more than extreme cold, thaw-freeze cycles (warm temperatures that cause melting followed by below-freezing temperatures that cause the wet to become ice) can make trails treacherous. Once the first frost hits, usually in late October but often earlier, traction aids like crampons, micro-spikes, and trekking poles become necessary equipment—as well as skill at winter hiking. An experienced winter hiking partner is not only a welcome companion in the mountains but also important for your safety.

Canine Compatibility

Canine compatibility describes whether dogs are allowed, whether it's advisable to bring dogs, and any considerations in regard to bringing your furry friend on the trail. In the Green Mountains, the things that make a route difficult or impossible for dogs are ladders up rock walls, rock chimneys without ladders, and terrain that requires rock hopping from boulder to boulder.

Many fabulous dog-friendly hikes in Vermont end at an old fire tower. Please avoid taking a dog up a fire tower! Dogs find the geometry and scaffolding confusing. For Fido's safety and yours, please leave your dog below on a lead. He couldn't care less about the view, but he might want to follow you up the tower's steep, narrow steps.

Some trailheads are located in state parks, which require dogs to be on leashes of 10 feet or less. You might have to show proof of rabies vaccine to enter a state park with a dog. Dogs should also be kept on a leash and on the trail in the alpine zone. Out of courtesy to other hikers, keep your dog under control at all times. Give hikers without dogs the right-of-way. If you meet another dog on the trail, quickly put your dog on a leash. And please pick up after your dog.

Trail Surface

Trail surface describes the material that makes up the trail. Many Green Mountain trails start on packed dirt and, as they gain elevation, become rockier. Often aids have been installed like ladders, steps, or handles. Some trails are better maintained than others. In a few instances, the hike follows a dirt road.

Land Status

All of the trails listed in this book—even those on privately owned land—are managed by a state or national agency, a local trail organization, or the Green Mountain Club and allow public access.

Nearest Amenities

If there are no amenities in close proximity to the general location of the trailhead, the nearest town with at least minimal amenities—that is, gas, food, and maybe lodging—is listed here. In small towns and villages, the hours these services are available may be limited. A best practice is to arrive at the trailhead with plenty of gas, food, and water.

Trail Users

This describes the other users that you might encounter on the hike. Mountain bikers and equestrians are the most common. Many of the hikes listed in this book are on Vermont's Long Trail, where hiking, snowshoeing, and skiing are the only modes of travel allowed.

Water Availability

Sources of water are listed if they are known to usually be reliable. In all cases, water obtained on a hike should be purified before use. The status of water sources can change due to weather, wildlife or livestock use, or other factors.

Maps

The maps in this guide are as accurate and current as possible. When used in conjunction with the hike description and the additional maps listed for each hike, you should have little trouble following the route.

USGS quads can usually be purchased at outdoor shops or ordered directly from the US Geological Survey at store.usgs.gov or from online companies such as www.mytopo.com or www.topozone.com. To order from the USGS, know the state, the exact map name as listed in the hike heading, and the scale.

Special Considerations

Permits are not usually required to hike on Vermont trails, and many organizations steward the trails and forests for the enjoyment and well-being of all. Some of the hikes in this book require a fee for entry, and some have special considerations. For example, they are on privately owned land and the landowner has a specific request. These considerations are listed with each hike where applicable.

Trail Contact

Many different agencies and organizations manage the hiking trails in the Green Mountains. The trail contact lists the name, phone number, and website of the managing agency for the lands through which the trail passes. Call or check the website for current information about the hike.

Finding the Trailhead

This section provides detailed directions to the trailhead. With a basic current state highway map or GPS unit, you can easily locate the starting point from the directions.

In general, the nearest town, or nearest intersection of main roads, is used as the starting point.

Distances were usually measured using a car odometer. Realize that different cars will vary slightly in their measurements. Even the same car will read slightly differently driving uphill on a dirt road versus downhill on a dirt road. Be sure to keep an eye open for the specific signs, junctions, and landmarks mentioned in the directions, not just the mileages. The map apps on cell phone GPS systems are often inaccurate or nonexistent in remote areas, so use them with care. In addition, many navigation apps require decent cell service to work, which might not exist where you are going.

All of the hikes in this guidebook have trailheads that can be reached by any vehicle without four-wheel drive.

Theft and vandalism can occur at trailheads. Try not to leave valuables in your car. If you must, lock them out of sight in the trunk. If you have room, put everything in the trunk to give the car an overall empty appearance.

The Hike

All of the hikes selected for this guide can be done by people in good physical condition. A little scrambling may be necessary, but none require technical rock-climbing skills.

The trails are mostly marked with blazes and sometimes rock cairns. Most of the time the paths are obvious, but the markers help when the trails are little used. Cairns are piles of rock built along the route. Tree blazes are I-shaped paintings on trees, usually at shoulder or head height. Blazes can be especially useful when a forest trail is obscured by snow. Be sure not to add your own blazes or cairns—it can confuse the route. Do volunteer to help your local nonprofit trail agency. Many of these markers are the result of the efforts of hiking enthusiasts like us, who gave their time and effort on organized trail maintenance days. Otherwise, leave such markings to official trail workers. Sometimes small plastic or aluminum markers are nailed to trees to mark the route.

If they're not on the trees, then check the ground for trail blazes. MARK AIKEN

Possible backcountry campsites may be suggested in the descriptions.

After reading the descriptions, pick the hike that most appeals to you. Go only as far as ability and desire allow. It's always okay to turn back. There is no obligation to complete any hike.

Miles and Directions

To help you stay on course, a detailed route finder gives the mileages of significant landmarks along the trail.

About the Maps

The overview map indicates major access roads to each trailhead and, possibly more important, the relative location of hikes to one another to help you plan a whole day or weekend of great hikes in one general vicinity.

For your own purposes, you may wish to copy the directions for the route onto a small sheet to help you while hiking, photocopy the map and Miles and Directions to take with you, or take a photo of one or both to save in your well-charged smartphone. Otherwise, just slip the whole book in your pack. Enjoy your time in the outdoors and remember to pack out what you pack in.

The route map is your guide to each hike. It shows the accessible roads and trails, water, landmarks, towns, and key navigational features. It also distinguishes trails from roads, and paved roads from unpaved roads. The selected route is highlighted.

The maps in this book are not intended to replace more-detailed agency maps, road maps, state atlases, and/or topographic maps, but they do indicate the general route to help you visualize and navigate its course.

Map Legend

Transportation

Interstate	═══◇═══ 15
US Highway	═══◇═══ 4
State Road	═══◇═══ 100
Local/Forest Road	═══USFS 21═══
Dirt Road	═ ═ ═ ═ ═
Railroad	├──┼──┼──┤
Featured Trail	▬▬▬▬▬
Other Trail	─ ─ ─ ─ ─ ─

Hydrology

Lake/Pond	
River/Brook	
Waterfall	

Land Use

State Park	

Symbols

Bench	▬
Boat Launch	⛵
Bridge	≍
Campground	⛺
Campsite (back country)	▲
City/Town	○
Pass/Gap	✕
Point of Interest	■
Mountain/Peak	▲
Parking	🅿
Picnic Area	🏕
Ranger Station	🏠
Steps	▥
Tower	🗼
Trailhead (start)	❶
Viewpoint	👁

Trail Finder

	Easy, Small Child Friendly	Dog Friendly	Cabins, Shelters	Tent Sites	Trailhead Campground	Open Rock or Alpine Summit	Rock Perch, Dramatic Cliff, or Ridge Walk	Lake, Pond	Waterfall	Fire Tower or Viewing Platform
SOUTHERN GREEN MOUNTAINS: Massachusetts Border to Londonderry										
1. Harmon Hill	●	●								
2. Haystack Mountain		●				●	●			
3. Stratton Mountain–Stratton Pond Loop		●	●	●				●		●
4. Bourn Pond–Stratton Pond Loop		●	●	●				●		
5. Lye Brook Falls	●	●							●	
6. Bromley Mountain		●	●							
SOUTH-CENTRAL GREEN MOUNTAINS: Danby to Killington										
7. Baker Peak–Griffith Lake Loop		●	●	●		●	●	●		
8. Okemo Mountain		●								●
9. Little Rock Pond and Green Mountain		●	●	●		●	●	●		
10. White Rocks Cliffs		●	●				●			
11. White Rocks Ice Beds	●						●		●	
12. Killington Peak		●	●			●				

13. Pico Peak	●	●	●						●
14. Deer Leap Outlook	●	●				●			
15. Blue Ridge Mountain	●					●		●	
NORTH-CENTRAL GREEN MOUNTAINS: Brandon Gap to Huntington									
16. Mount Horrid's Great Cliffs	●					●			
17. Silver Lake	●		●	●			●		
18. Rattlesnake Cliffs and Mount Moosalamoo	●		●	●		●		●	
19. Abbey Pond	●						●		
20. Mount Abraham via the Long Trail	●	●			●				
21. Mount Abraham via the Battell Trail	●	●			●				
22. Mount Ellen	●					●			
23. Mount Philo	●		●			●			
WATERBURY-STOWE AREA: Waterbury to Jeffersonville									
24. Camel's Hump via the Monroe Trail	●				●	●			
25. Camel's Hump via the Forest City Trail–Burrows Trail Loop	●	●			●	●			
26. Stimson Mountain	●					●			

	Easy, Small Child Friendly	Dog Friendly	Cabins, Shelters	Tent Sites	Trailhead Campground	Open Rock or Alpine Summit	Rock Perch, Dramatic Cliff, or Ridge Walk	Lake, Pond	Waterfall	Fire Tower or Viewing Platform
27. Mount Hunger with White Rock option		•				•				
28. Stowe Pinnacle	•	•				•				
29. Mount Elmore and Balanced Rock		•		•	•					•
30. Mount Mansfield: The Forehead via the Butler Lodge Trail–Maple Ridge Loop			•			•	•			
31. Mount Mansfield via the Sunset Ridge Trail		•			•	•	•			
32. Mount Mansfield via the Long Trail-South			•			•	•			
33. Elephant's Head Cliff–Sterling Pond Loop			•				•	•		
34. Devil's Gulch–Ritterbush Pond Loop			•				•	•		
35. Belvidere Mountain Loop		•	•					•		•
36. Wheeler Mountain		•					•			
37. Mount Pisgah	•	•	•				•	•		
38. Bald Mountain (Westmore)	•	•	•							•
39. Bluff Mountain Loop			•				•			
40. Jay Peak	•	•				•	•			

Southern Green Mountains

Massachusetts Border to Londonderry

1 Harmon Hill via the Appalachian Trail/Long Trail

Popular trek through an airy hardwood forest to a landmark on the Appalachian Trail, with views of the nearby Bennington area and Taconic Range to the west. Wild-flowers in May include trout lily (dog-toothed violet), squirrel corn, spring beauties, purple trillium, hobblebush, yellow violets, and bellwort.

General location: Bennington
Distance: 3.4 miles out and back
Hiking time: About 3 hours
Highest point: 2,325 feet
Elevation gain: 1,265 feet
Difficulty: Moderate
When to go: Year-round, except during mud season
Canine compatibility: Dog friendly. Dogs should be under control at all times and on leash around other hikers.
Trail surface: Dirt path, stone steps
Land status: Public

Trail users: Hikers only
Water availability: No reliable water, though the riverlike City Stream flows past the parking lot, offering a refreshing spot for your dog to cool off after the hike.
Maps: USGS Woodford, Bennington, Pownal quads
Special considerations: None
Trail contact: Green Mountain Club, (802) 244-7037, www.greenmountainclub.org; Green Mountain National Forest, Manchester District, (802) 362-2307, www.fs.usda.gov/gmfl

Finding the trailhead: From the junction of US 7 and Route 9 in Bennington, travel east on Route 9 toward Wilmington for 4.9 miles. Trailhead parking is on the north (left) side of the road. Cross the road to the trailhead for the Appalachian Trail (AT)/Long Trail (LT)–South. From the junction of Routes 9 and 100 in Wilmington, travel west on Route 9 for 15.5 miles. Trailhead parking is on the right side of the road.

The Hike

Harmon Hill was likely named for the prominent Harmon family of the town of Rupert in Bennington County. Reuben Harmon Jr., a member of the Vermont General Assembly, was authorized to mine and mint copper coins in this region as part of Vermont's proclamation as an independent republic prior to its becoming the fourteenth state in 1791.

The climb up Harmon Hill starts out with a cardio bang, but ends with a casual lilt. While the views from the summit are not particularly dramatic, it is a pleasing destination at the end of a nice woodland walk.

Enter the woods on the AT/LT–South (white blazes). The path climbs steeply up a long series of stone steps and well-placed rocks, in a show of expert trail work, and gains elevation quickly. By 0.2 mile it levels off and bends right (west), continuing upward but in a series of waves and at a more moderate incline.

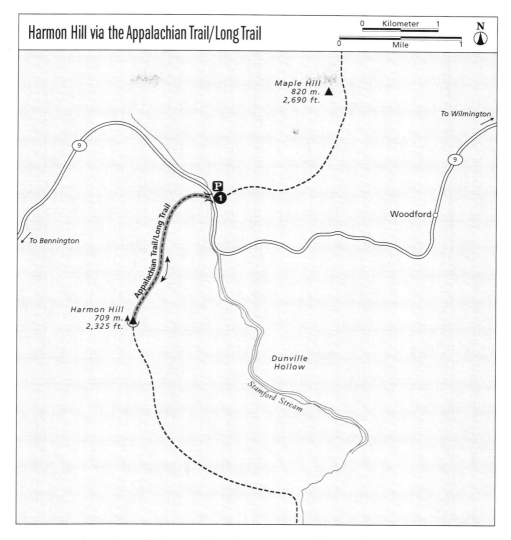

At about 0.4 mile the trail bends back to the left (south). It then heads upward through the hardwood forest via several elongated switchbacks with rock steps in steeper sections.

By 0.8 mile the trail crests a plateau, then meanders in a westerly direction, slightly downhill, and crosses a narrow streamlet. The footing is noticeably smoother. In May the woods here are carpeted with yellow trout lilies (also called dog-toothed violets), with their mottled green and brown leaves.

At about 1.2 miles the trail bends left (south) again, crossing a series of puncheons over a muddy area. From here it climbs gently for the remainder of the route. Spring beauties take over as the dominant ground cover under the trees. Their small white and pink flowers cause the forest floor to shimmer when they bloom during the spring.

The trail reaches the summit of Harmon Hill at 1.7 miles. A green box marks the end of the Pioneer Valley section of the Long Trail and the start of the Bennington section. (*Note:* The Pioneer Valley section of the LT disbanded in 1994, so it stands to reason that this sign will eventually be replaced.) The sign also notes the three-quarter point of the Appalachian Trail, 1,563 miles from Springer Mountain, Georgia, and 557 miles to Mount Katadin, Maine. Char marks on some of the trees are evidence of the periodic controlled burns by the Forest Service to help maintain the grassy summit.

From the sign, grassy paths fan out in each direction, revealing views of nearby hills. The view to the west is the best of nearby Mount Anthony and the Taconic Range beyond, the Bennington area, and the towering monument commemorating the Revolutionary War Battle of Bennington in 1777.

Return by the same route.

Miles and Directions

0.0 Start at the trailhead for the AT/LT–South. Climb steeply up a rocky slope.

0.2 Level off briefly, bending to the west. Continue to climb in waves.

0.4 Bend back south, ascending elongated switchbacks.

0.8 Reach a plateau. Footing becomes smoother through an airy hardwood forest in a predominantly westward direction.

1.2 Bend south again, crossing a series of puncheons.

1.7 SUMMIT! Marked by a sign and a green box. Return by the same route.

3.4 Arrive back at the trailhead.

◀ *Harmon Hill puncheon.* LISA BALLARD

2 Haystack Mountain via the Deerfield Ridge Trail

A pleasant, gradual climb to a small rocky summit with excellent views, especially to the east into New Hampshire. The rocky perch at the summit over Haystack Pond is a perfect picnic spot.

General location: Wilmington
Distance: 4.8 miles out and back
Hiking time: About 3.5 hours
Highest point: 3,420 feet
Elevation gain: 1,020 feet
Difficulty: Moderate
When to go: Year-round, except during mud season
Canine compatibility: Dog friendly. Excellent route for puppies and senior dogs. Carry water.
Trail surface: Dirt path, some rocks

Land status: Public
Trail users: Mostly hikers; however, it is a multiuse trail.
Water availability: None
Map: USGS Mount Snow quad
Special considerations: None
Trail contact: Green Mountain Club, (802) 244-7037, www.greenmountainclub.org; Green Mountain National Forest, Manchester District, (802) 362-2307, www.fs.usda.gov/gmfl

Finding the trailhead: From Route 9 west of Wilmington, turn right onto Chimney Hill Road. Turn right on Binney Brook Road and follow it uphill through a residential development. Turn left on Upper Dam Road. The trailhead and parking are on the right.

The Hike

Haystack Mountain is a common name for peaks in the Northeast. The name comes from the mountain's shape, which resembles a giant stack of hay. During the 1800s much of Vermont's woodlands were cleared for farming. While most of those fields have grown back into forest, and the remaining farmers now make large bales instead of stacks of hay, the mountains of that shape remain as a reminder of this heritage.

There are three Haystack Mountains with hiking trails in Vermont. Two are in the Northeast Kingdom, one near Jay Peak and one near Lake Willoughby. The third, described here, is at the opposite end of the state near Mount Snow.

This Haystack Mountain is well-known among the region's skiers as a struggling satellite ski area to giant Mount Snow. From a hiker's point of view, whatever Haystack lacks as a ski area, it more than makes up for as a hiking destination. While Mount Snow is bigger, its trail system is popular for mountain biking. The Deerfield Ridge Trail (blue blazes) is also sometimes known as the Haystack Mountain Trail. Most current signage says "Deerfield Ridge Trail." It is named for another section of the multiuse trail between Haystack and Mount Snow that traverses Deerfield Ridge. The hike described here is only to the top of Haystack and is mainly used as a footpath. It is thus more conducive to an invigorating yet peaceful walk in the woods.

View of Haystack Pond from the summit of Haystack Mountain Lisa Ballard

The trail begins on a gravel road. Walk around the gate partway up the initial incline, continuing along the road.

At 0.4 mile the trail turns left over a streamlet onto a wide footpath, leaving the woods road behind. After descending through a muddy area, the path ascends gently through hardwoods and then flattens out, heading north.

At 1.0 mile the trail resumes its gentle ascent, bending to the right. *Note:* The trail markers in this section are plastic blue diamonds rather than the painted vertical rectangles more common to Vermont's trails.

At 1.6 miles the trail comes to another plateau. The canopy opens up over the trail as it passes through a hedge of wild blackberry bushes. A little while later, it crosses another muddy area, then ascends gently again. The trail becomes rockier, with water trickling down it unless the weather has been unusually dry.

At 2.0 miles a small rock cairn blocks the middle of the trail, and a yellow arrow signals a 90-degree turn to the right up a short, steep incline. The trail soon moderates again, winding up the hill.

At 2.4 miles the trail comes to a large rock as hardwoods give way to firs. Scramble over it to the top! Haystack Pond lies about 500 feet below the summit, with Mount Monadnock in New Hampshire directly ahead to the east. The Mount Snow ski area is obvious to the left (north). On a clear day, Killington and the Coolidge Range are also visible to the north beyond Mount Snow. Wachusett Mountain and Greylock in Massachusetts lie on the southern horizon.

Return by the same route.

Haystack Mountain via Deerfield Ridge Trail

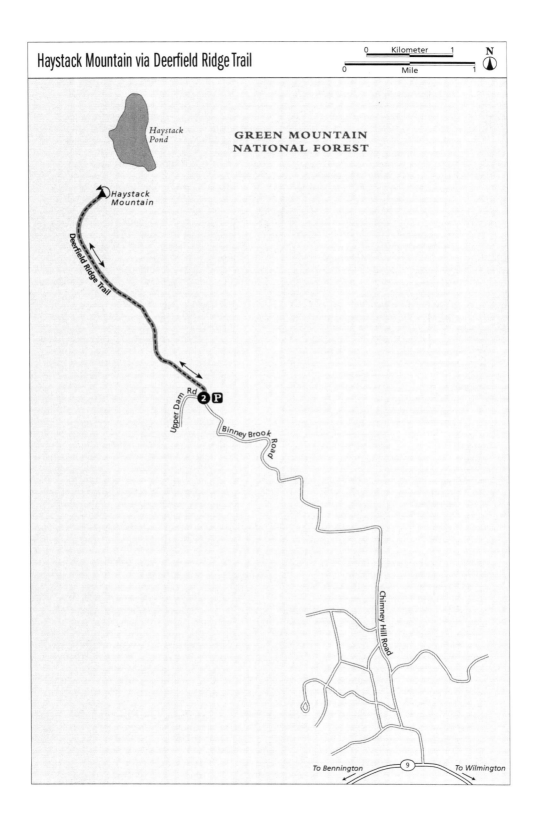

Miles and Directions

0.0   Start at the Haystack Mountain/Deerfield Ridge trailhead. Walk around the gate on a gravel road.

0.4   Turn left off the gravel road onto a wide footpath, which becomes flat after an initial moderate ascent.

1.0   Resume a gentle ascent.

1.6   Traverse a plateau. Break in the forest canopy.

2.0   Turn right at the rock cairn up a short, steep incline.

2.4   SUMMIT! Return by the same route.

4.8   Arrive back at the trailhead.

3 Stratton Mountain–Stratton Pond Loop

A long day hike or overnight backpacking trip over the tallest peak in southern Vermont and by the largest body of water on the Long Trail. The historic fire tower on the summit of Stratton offers a sweeping 360-degree view.

General location: Stratton
Distance: 11.5-mile loop
Hiking time: About 8 hours (day hike); 2 days (backpacking)
Highest point: 3,936 feet
Elevation gain: 1,910 feet
Difficulty: Very strenuous day hike (due to mileage); moderate backpacking trip
When to go: Year-round, except during mud season
Canine compatibility: Dog friendly

Trail surface: Packed dirt, rocks
Land status: Public
Trail users: Hikers, snowshoers
Water availability: Pond
Map: USGS Stratton quad
Special considerations: None
Trail contact: Green Mountain Club, (802) 244-7037, www.greenmountainclub.org; Green Mountain National Forest, Manchester District, (802) 362-2307, www.fs.usda.gov/gmfl

Finding the trailhead: From the village of Stratton—not the ski resort—drive 3 miles west toward Arlington on Stratton-Arlington Road/Kelley Stand Road (closed in winter). The trailhead for the Appalachian Trail/Long Trail (AT/LT) is on the north side of the road just past the trailhead for Grout Pond.

The Hike

The Stratton Mountain–Stratton Pond Loop is one of Vermont's classic hiking routes. While it is lengthy mileage-wise as a day hike, the footing is generally good and the elevation gain reasonable for the distance. However, if you have the time, it's worth planning a night by Stratton Pond either in the shelter or at one of the tent sites. The 46-acre pond is like a small lake and an endless source of backcountry entertainment. You can take a dip, go fishing for brook trout or bullhead, or simply relax by your tent as you listen to the waves gently lap the shoreline.

The elevation gain on the loop is up Stratton Mountain, which is of historical significance to hikers. It was atop Stratton Mountain in 1921 that Benton MacKaye first conceived of the Appalachian Trail, from Georgia to Maine. His inspiration came from another hiker, James Taylor, who in 1909 first proposed a "long trail" to link the main peaks of the Green Mountains along the entire length of Vermont. A significant portion of the Stratton Mountain–Stratton Pond Loop is on the AT/LT (white blazes).

From the trailhead on Kelley Stand Road, follow the AT/LT–North into the woods. The trail comes immediately to a fork. Bear right, traversing a muddy area.

Fire tower atop Stratton Mountain. Lisa Ballard

At 0.4 mile the trail crosses a streamlet and starts to climb easily along a woods road. It crosses several stretches of puncheons as it traverses slightly downhill, heading toward the mountain. Watch the white blazes carefully, as many old logging roads crisscross the trail here.

At 1.2 miles the trail bends to the right (east) and climbs gently again over a knoll. It crosses several streamlets as it dips and bends, alternating between mellow climbing and flat walking.

At 1.9 miles the climb becomes more persistent and rockier before flattening out again. The trail travels along a hillside, generally heading northward.

By 2.9 miles the trail reaches an upland plateau. The trees become noticeably lower and thinner, and softwoods take over. The miles go by quickly on this low-angle ascent. Nothing about the trail is steep or tricky. By 3.6 miles the trail gets rockier again.

At 3.8 miles the trail passes a white cabin on the summit of Stratton Mountain, which is reserved for a caretaker from the Green Mountain Club. The fire tower is directly ahead at the other end of the grassy clearing. Built in 1914, the original cabin atop the tower was replaced in 1934 with the current one. The Stratton fire tower is a designated National Historic Landmark. From its small metal cabin, 55 feet above the ground, you can see the top of the ski area's gondola, 0.8 mile away on Stratton's north peak. The view from the tower extends into five states. Mount Snow is clearly visible to the south. Mount Monadnock in New Hampshire lies to the southeast, with Mount Ascutney to the northeast and Mount Equinox to the west. Stratton Pond is below to the northwest.

From the base of the fire tower, turn left and begin the descent toward Stratton Pond. At 4.1 miles the trail bends to the left down wooden steps as it winds off the peak and reenters the hardwoods.

At 5.8 miles the trail bends to the west, then crosses a logging road. It traverses a long, muddy area, eventually crossing a stream on a bridge. From the bridge, it climbs gently to a fork with an older trail. Bear right at the fork, heading uphill.

At 6.8 miles the trail comes to the junction with the Stratton Pond Trail. Turn right toward Stratton Pond, continuing on the AT/LT–North a short way to the water's edge. Stratton Pond receives the heaviest use of any body of water on the Long Trail, particularly during the summer. However, if you trek there midweek after Labor Day, you'll likely be alone. Camping is allowed at nearby Stratton Pond Shelter and designated tent sites. There is a small nightly fee per person, which helps defray the costs of managing the AT/LT in Vermont. The Green Mountain Club stations a caretaker at a clearing at the pond's edge during the summer, not only to collect camping fees but also to maintain trails, compost sewage, and educate people about the area and how to be a low-impact hiker.

From Stratton Pond, backtrack the short distance to the junction of the AT/LT and the Stratton Pond Trail, continuing straight ahead on the Stratton Pond Trail (blue blazes). At the top of the next rise, the trail turns right, then bends right past

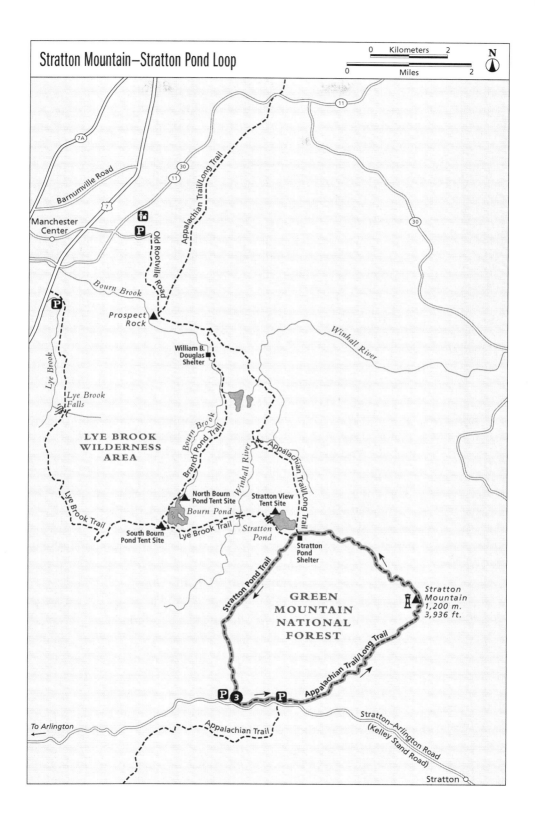

Stratton Mountain–Stratton Pond Loop

Kilometers 0 — 2

Miles 0 — 2

N

7A

Barnumville Road

7

11

30

Appalachian Trail/Long Trail

Manchester Center

P

Old Rootville Road

Bourn Brook

P

Prospect Rock

Lye Brook

Lye Brook Falls

William B. Douglas Shelter

Winhall River

30

LYE BROOK WILDERNESS AREA

Bourn Brook

Branch Pond Trail

Winhall River

Appalachian Trail/Long Trail

Lye Brook Trail

North Bourn Pond Tent Site

Bourn Pond

Stratton View Tent Site

South Bourn Pond Tent Site

Lye Brook Trail

Stratton Pond

Stratton Pond Shelter

Stratton Pond Trail

GREEN MOUNTAIN NATIONAL FOREST

Stratton Mountain 1,200 m. 3,936 ft.

Appalachian Trail/Long Trail

P 3

P

Appalachian Trail/Long Trail

To Arlington

Appalachian Trail

Stratton-Arlington Road (Kelley Stand Road)

Stratton

the short spur to Stratton Pond Shelter (straight ahead). Built in 1999, the shelter is an oversize lean-to, open on one side, with bunk platforms and a sleeping loft above a picnic table.

Beyond this spur, ignore the intersection with the Lye Brook Trail, which heads to the right (west). At 7.9 miles the trail crosses the first of many puncheons as it heads gently downward.

At 9.0 miles the trail crosses a woods road, then continues its long traverse over more puncheons, finally reaching Kelley Stand Road at 10.6 miles, though not your car. Turn left (east) and walk along the dirt road for another 0.9 mile, closing the loop where you started at the AT/LT trailhead.

Miles and Directions

0.0 Start at the trailhead for the AT/LT–North. Bear right at the fork, traversing a muddy area.

0.4 Cross a streamlet and then begin a gentle climb on a woods road.

1.2 Bend east, climbing over a knoll.

1.9 Climb more persistently, then level off, heading northward.

2.9 Reach a plateau. The trees get smaller, with more softwoods.

3.6 The trail becomes noticeably rockier.

3.8 SUMMIT! Pass by the caretaker's cabin to reach the fire tower. Turn left (northwest) at the fire tower and begin the descent to Stratton Pond.

5.8 Bend west, crossing a logging road.

6.8 POND! Turn right at the junction with the Stratton Pond Trail, staying on the AT/LT–North a short way to the shoreline of Stratton Pond. Retrace the short distance back to the junction with the Stratton Pond Trail. Head south on the Stratton Pond Trail.

7.9 Traverse the first of many puncheons.

9.0 Cross a woods road and then traverse more puncheons.

10.6 Turn left (east) onto Kelley Stand Road.

11.5 Close the loop at your starting point, the trailhead for the AT/LT–North.

4 Bourn Pond–Stratton Pond Loop

Overnight backpacking on wooded rolling terrain past two ponds, followed by a long, peaceful forest walk through the Lye Brook Wilderness.

General location: Manchester
Distance: 17.3-mile lollipop
Hiking time: 2–3 days
Highest point: 2,250 feet
Elevation gain: 1,165 feet
Difficulty: Moderate
When to go: Year-round, except during mud season
Canine compatibility: Dog friendly
Trail surface: Packed dirt, some rocks, mud, plenty of puncheons
Land status: Public

Trail users: Hikers, snowshoers
Water availability: Bourn Pond, Stratton Pond, and lots of stream crossings. There's a spring at Stratton View tent site.
Maps: USGS Stratton Mountain, Sunderland, Peru, and Manchester quads
Special considerations: There is a nominal camping fee at Stratton View tent site.
Trail contact: Green Mountain Club, (802) 244-7037, www.greenmountainclub.org; Green Mountain National Forest, Manchester District, (802) 362-2307, www.fs.usda.gov/gmfl

Finding the trailhead: From exit 4 on US 7, follow Route 30/11 east for 0.5 mile. Turn right onto East Manchester Road, then immediately bear left on Old Rootville Road (dirt). Go 0.5 mile to the end of the drivable portion of the road. The small turnout on the right beneath a gigantic water tank is the trailhead parking area. If there are no spots in the turnout, park on the roadside beneath the turnout; there is no roadside parking allowed between the turnout and the trailhead.

The Hike

The hike to Bourn Pond and Stratton Pond is an excellent way to traverse through the heart of the Lye Brook Wilderness. There are lengthy stretches through pristine woodlands on this trek, but the big rewards are an early view from Prospect Rock above Manchester and then your choice of shelters or pondside tent sites. This loop hike is described here as a two-day outing, but many extend it to three days (or longer), base camping at either Bourn Pond or Stratton Pond and then using the extra day to either climb Stratton Mountain or just enjoy some swimming and fishing.

Day One

From the parking area, head up the gravel continuation of Old Rootville Road, aka Prospect Rock Trail, passing the sign for the Green Mountain National Forest. The road ascends an unrelenting 1,000 feet, paralleling Bourn Brook on your right.

At about 1.5 miles the road levels off. You can glimpse Mount Equinox and the Taconic Range to your right (west) through the trees.

At 1.8 miles the Prospect Rock Trail ends at the Appalachian Trail/Long Trail (AT/LT; white blazes). The AT/LT–North departs the road to the left, and the road becomes the AT/LT–South. It's easy to miss the short spur to Prospect Rock (blue blazes), which is on the right, as the sign announcing this rocky perch is about 15 feet high on a white birch tree. The sign at eye level merely says "Look Up." Prospect Rock is a popular destination in its own right for those short on time but who want a nice view. The hulking Mount Equinox is directly across the Otter Creek Valley, a large section of which lies before you to the north.

From Prospect Rock, continue up the road, soon coming to a gate at 2.4 miles on which there's a sign advising hikers that if they were looking for Prospect Rock, they missed it. Walk around the gate and follow the road until it takes a sharp bend to the left up a steep incline. Ignore the turn and head straight into the woods onto a footpath. Fifty yards later, you'll come to an unofficial junction. Continue straight ahead on the AT/LT–South, ignoring the overgrown snowmobile trail on the left.

At 2.7 miles the trail crosses a tributary of Bourn Brook. The footbridge is closed for repairs as of this writing. According to the Green Mountain Club (GMC), it's on their to-do list, but the completion date is unknown. Follow the trail across the deep but dry streambed and ascend a small rise to the junction with the Branch Pond Trail. You will close the loop at this intersection tomorrow.

Bear right (south) on the Branch Pond Trail and pass a sign marking the boundary of the Lye Brook Wilderness. The route crosses puncheons as it traverses through the hardwood forest, with a jewelweed carpet on either side of the boards. After a long, gradual descent, the trail crosses more puncheons and then arrives at Douglas Shelter at 3.2 miles. The shelter is a typical three-sided lean-to in a small clearing. It was built in 1956 and renovated in 2005. If you are planning a couple nights in the Lye Brook Wilderness and get a late start, this is a good place to sleep the first night.

The trail crosses the front of the shelter and then heads southeast back into the woods. From here it is a pleasant, rolling 3-mile walk through the woods to Bourn Pond. The trail passes through a small clearing filled with head-high goldenrod. It is lesser used than the AT/LT and is prime moose habitat. Constant signs of these large ungulates can be found here, including hand-size hoofprints and scat. At one point the trail dips down to a stream, then continues along its left bank. Farther along there are a couple of unaided stream crossings, as bridges are generally not constructed in designated wilderness areas.

At 6.2 miles the trail reaches the northern end of Bourn Pond, which is visible across the marsh grass through the trees. The trail generally follows the western shoreline of the pond, though it swings away from the water briefly on old log ties until it meets the spur to the North Bourn Pond tent site. Continue straight on the Branch Pond Trail–South. Moments later, the trail comes alongside the water, soon passing a couple of beautiful pondside tent sites.

At 6.7 miles the Branch Pond Trail meets the Lye Brook Trail, which enters from the right (west). The site of the former South Bourn Pond Shelter, now a primitive campsite, is also just to the right. The two trails run concurrently to the left (east) for about 50 yards, then the Branch Pond Trail splits off to the right, continuing south. Stay on the Lye Brook Trail, heading east.

At 7.7 miles the forest's personality shifts due to a microburst in 2006, which created an expansive blowdown. Since then, scrub and head-high vegetation have taken over. The trail makes its way through the blowdown, where wild raspberry bushes abound among the jumble of tree trunks. At the opposite side of the microburst, the trail crosses a small backwater. The footing on this crossing is tricky across fallen debris. This part of the trail is a work in progress, according to the GMC, and will likely change. On the other side of the crossing, the trail passes out of the Lye Brook Wilderness.

The trail reenters the forest and then turns sharply left (west) where a small footbridge used to cross a stream. The splintered bridge is buried in debris to the left, but you can still easily step across the water. From there, the route climbs a low hillside,

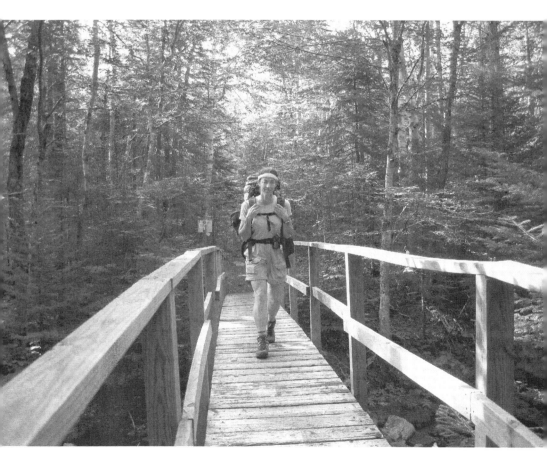

Lisa Ballard on the bridge across the Winhall River in the Lye Brook Wilderness. LISA BALLARD

reaching the corner of Stratton Pond at 8.6 miles. Here, a spur heads left along the northern shoreline of Stratton Pond to the Stratton View tent site. The trail passes the water source for the tent site and a small grassy opening on the shore of the pond, which is the best access into the water for a swim. The top of Stratton Mountain's gondola and the fire tower sit like two crowns on the elongated peak on the opposite shoreline. Listen for the call of the loons and watch for a brook trout rising on the water.

The Stratton View site has several tent platforms available on a first-come, first-served basis. Expect a caretaker from the Green Mountain Club to visit during the summer and early fall to exchange pleasantries about your hike and to collect the site fee; the charge is per person. There's also a fire pit for a campfire.

Day Two

In prior years, the trail continued around the northern shoreline of Stratton Pond, but—despite the cancellation of many work projects due to the COVID-19 pandemic—in the summer of 2020 GMC work crews donned hard hats and facial coverings to complete significant trail rerouting on all sides of the pond in order to preserve the fragile shoreline ecosystems. From the tent site, retrace your steps back to the Lye Brook Trail. Turn left and immediately cross the pond's outlet on 100 feet of elevated boardwalk.

The Lye Brook Trail continues for a quarter mile over puncheons along the pond's edge before veering uphill and away from the pond until it meets the Stratton Pond Trail at 9.5 miles. Turn left (north) back in the direction of the pond, ignoring a spur trail that comes in from the right (south). At 9.7 miles reunite with the AT/LT and turn left (north).

The AT/LT passes the GMC caretaker's tent site at the southeastern corner of the pond before following the eastern shoreline and then heading back into the forest at 10.1 miles. The AT/LT passes the Catamount ski trail on the right and reenters the Lye Brook Wilderness. From here it rolls at length through the airy forest.

At about 11.7 miles the forest monotony is broken by a well-constructed footbridge over the Winhall River. At 12.9 miles the trail takes a noticeable turn to the left (west) at a low, viewless pinnacle in the woods. At 13.1 miles it comes to a rocky double stream crossing, with stone stairs up the far bank.

After several stretches of puncheons, the loop finally closes at the junction with the Branch Pond Trail at 14.6 miles. From here, retrace back to the Old Rootville Road/Prospect Rock Trail, passing Prospect Rock and descending back to the trailhead at 17.3 miles.

Miles and Directions

0.0   Start at the trailhead for the Prospect Rock Trail on Old Rootville Road.

1.8   PROSPECT ROCK! The AT/LT-North departs to the left; a short spur to Prospect Rock is on the right. Continue up the road, now the AT/LT-South.

Bourn Pond–Stratton Pond Loop

Kilometers

Miles

N

Manchester Center

30

11

7

P

4

Old Rootville Road

Appalachian Trail/Long Trail

Bourn Brook

P

Prospect Rock

William B. Douglas Shelter

Winhall River

Lye Brook

Lye Brook Falls

LYE BROOK WILDERNESS AREA

Lye Brook Trail

Branch Pond Trail

Bourn Brook

Appalachian Trail/Long Trail

Winhall River

North Bourn Pond Tent Site

Bourn Pond

Stratton View Tent Site

Lye Brook Trail

South Bourn Pond Tent Site

Stratton Pond

Stratton Shelter

Stratton Pond Trail

GREEN MOUNTAIN NATIONAL FOREST

Stratton Mountain 1,200 m. 3,936 ft.

P

P

Appalachian Trail/Long Trail

Stratton–Arlington Road (Kelley Stand Road)

To Arlington

To Stratton

2.7 Bear right (south) at the junction of the AT/LT and Branch Pond Trail onto the Branch Pond Trail.

3.2 Pass Douglas Shelter. Stay here if you had a late start.

6.2 BOURN POND! Reach the North Bourn Pond tent site.

6.7 Junction with the Lye Brook Trail. The South Bourn Pond tent site is on the right. Turn left onto the Lye Brook Trail, heading east.

8.6 STRATTON POND! Turn left (east) onto the spur along the Stratton Pond shoreline to the Stratton View tent site. Stay here, then retrace your steps back to the Lye Brook Trail in the morning.

9.5 Turn left on the Stratton Pond Trail.

9.7 Turn left on the AT/LT.

14.6 Close the loop at the junction with the Branch Pond Trail.

15.5 Pass by Prospect Rock again. Follow the Old Rootville Road downhill, back to the trailhead.

17.3 Arrive back at the trailhead.

5 Lye Brook Falls

A serene woodland walk to a spectacular 160-foot waterfall, one of the tallest in Vermont.

General location: Manchester
Distance: 4.6 miles out and back
Hiking time: About 3.5 hours
Highest point: 1,350 feet
Elevation gain: 1,000 feet
Difficulty: Moderate
When to go: Year-round
Canine compatibility: Dog friendly. Keep dogs on a short leash near the cliffs around the waterfall.
Trail surface: Smooth, packed dirt

Land status: Public
Trail users: Hikers, snowshoers
Water availability: Unreliable, except at falls, but water collection there would be challenging.
Map: USGS Manchester quad
Special considerations: None
Trail contact: Green Mountain Club, (802) 244-7037, www.greenmountainclub.org; Green Mountain National Forest, Manchester Office, (802) 362-2307, www.fs.usda.gov/gmfl

Finding the trailhead: From US 7 in Manchester, take Route 30/11 east for 0.4 mile. Take a hard right (southwest) on East Manchester Road. Go 1.2 miles and turn left (south) on Glen Road. Glen Road immediately crosses a bridge, turns to dirt, and comes to a fork. Bear right at the fork nearest the "Lye Brook Wilderness Entry 7" sign. Continue 0.4 mile to a dead-end circle. The trailhead is on the southeastern side of the circle.

The Hike

The route to Lye Brook Falls along the Lye Brook Trail (blue blazes) is a wonderful half-day introduction to hiking. The trail is broad and follows an old logging road and a railroad bed. It climbs gently, gaining about 800 feet from the trailhead to the spur to the falls, passing through peaceful forest. It then drops 200 feet on a moderate incline to the falls. Save this hike for after a rainstorm, as the falls dry to a less-impressive trickle by mid-June.

From the trailhead, the trail forks after a hundred feet. Straight goes to a view of the streambed. Bear left, following an arrow sign deeply embedded in a maple tree. The path starts out over giant cobblestone-like rocks, but after a few moments, it bends to the right (south) and becomes a smooth woods road.

At about 0.4 mile the trail passes a washout where you can see Lye Brook at the bottom of the steep, eroded bank. The sign-in box for the Lye Brook Wilderness Area is around the bend, at 0.5 mile. Sign in, then continue around another bend to find an unusually long, straight corridor. The rest of the route follows this former railroad bed, which was used for logging. Years ago, the tracks passed the base of Lye Brook Falls on a trestle, hence the original name of the waterfall, Trestle Falls.

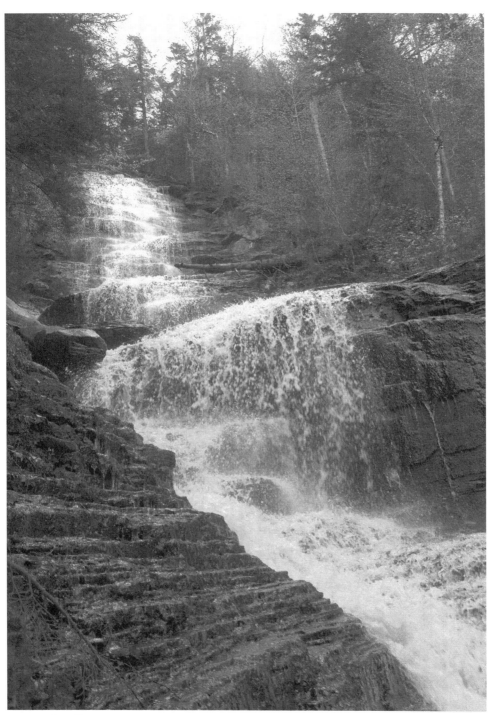

Lye Brook Falls. LISA BALLARD

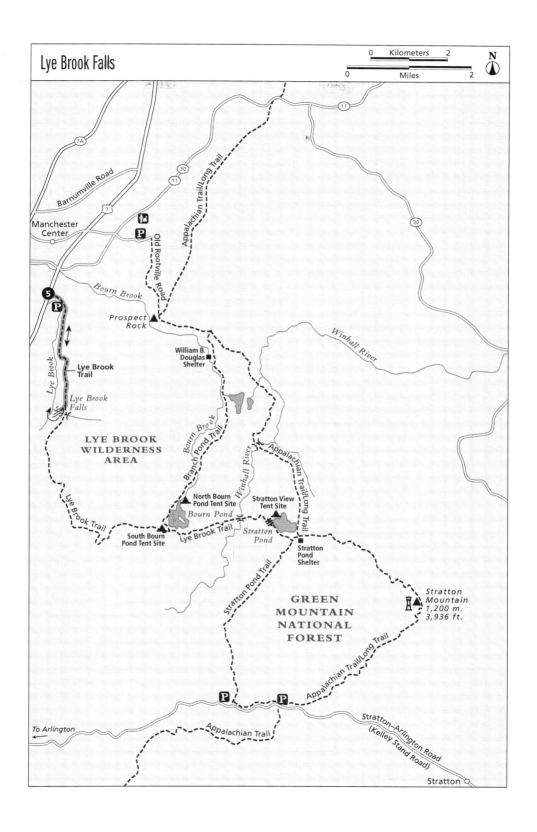

Lye Brook Falls

Kilometers

Miles

N

Barnumville Road

7A

7

Manchester Center

Old Rootville Road

Appalachian Trail/Long Trail

11

30

11

30

Bourn Brook

5

P

Lye Brook Trail

Lye Brook

Lye Brook Falls

Prospect Rock

William B. Douglas Shelter

Winhall River

LYE BROOK WILDERNESS AREA

Bourn Brook

Branch Pond Trail

Winhall River

Appalachian Trail/Long Trail

North Bourn Pond Tent Site

Bourn Pond

Stratton View Tent Site

South Bourn Pond Tent Site

Lye Brook Trail

Lye Brook Trail

Stratton Pond

Stratton Pond Shelter

Stratton Pond Trail

GREEN MOUNTAIN NATIONAL FOREST

Stratton Mountain 1,200 m. 3,936 ft.

Appalachian Trail/Long Trail

P

P

Appalachian Trail/Long Trail

To Arlington

Appalachian Trail

Stratton–Arlington Road (Kelley Stand Road)

Stratton

At 0.6 mile the trail crosses the first of two streamlets, then begins to climb noticeably uphill. The tree branches close in along this section of the trail.

At 1.3 miles the trail bends left (northeast) over a substantial rock water bar, then winds back to its original direction. At the top of the rise is another double stream crossing, between which the path seems like a rocky streambed itself.

After the second streamlet, the trail levels off, passing through a stand of hemlocks as it traverses the side of Lye Brook Hollow, a shallow ravine. The hillside above looks like an overgrown scree field, though the path underfoot is smooth.

At 1.8 miles the trail crosses a slightly wider stream on large rocks and then comes to the junction with the spur to Lye Brook Falls. Bear right (southwest) at the fork. The trail feels slightly narrower as it heads downhill, dropping down the side of the ravine, but it is a continuation of the same railroad bed. This section sustained significant damage during Tropical Storm Irene in 2011 but was repaired by Green Mountain Club trail crews. After rain, sections of the trail can be rather wet where water flows off the rock outcroppings beside the path. At 2.0 miles the trail crosses a rockslide.

The official spur trail ends at a rocky perch over the base of Lye Brook Falls at 2.3 miles. You can climb partway up the left side of the cascade via a narrow path that passes another rocky perch, an excellent place to view the tumbling white water apart from other visitors on the larger rock below. Most of the year, the falls are not a raging torrent. The water flows down the rocks like a broad layer of white satin coating a hundred steps, which is what makes this such a beautiful, relaxing place to visit.

Return by the same route.

Miles and Directions

0.0   Start at the trailhead for the Lye Brook Trail. Climb over large cobble-like rocks.

0.4   Pass a washout with a view of Lye Brook below.

0.5   Sign in at the boundary of the Lye Brook Wilderness Area.

0.6   Cross two streamlets, then climb more noticeably uphill.

1.3   Turn left (northeast) over a substantial rock water bar, then cross two more streamlets at the top of the rise.

1.8   Cross a wider stream on mossy rocks. Bear right at the fork onto the spur trail to Lye Brook Falls, heading downhill.

2.0   Cross a rockslide.

2.3   WATERFALL! Return by the same route.

4.6   Arrive back at the trailhead.

6 Bromley Mountain via the Appalachian Trail/Long Trail

A gradual yet steady climb through a hardwood forest to the top of the Bromley Ski Area. Pass one of the newer lodges on the Appalachian Trail/Long Trail (AT/LT) in Vermont. Excellent views, particularly toward Stratton to the south.

General location: Peru

Distance: 5.6 miles out and back

Hiking time: About 4.5 hours

Highest point: 3,260 feet

Elevation gain: 1,460 feet

Difficulty: More challenging

When to go: Year-round, except during mud season

Canine compatibility: Dog friendly

Trail surface: Dirt path changing to grassy or snowy, depending on the season

Land status: Public

Trail users: Hikers only, though in winter the top of this hike is a ski trail.

Water availability: Unreliable

Map: USGS Peru quad

Special considerations: None

Trail contact: Green Mountain Club, (802) 244-7037, www.greenmountainclub.org; Green Mountain National Forest, Manchester District, (802) 362-2307, www.fs.usda.gov/gmfl

Finding the trailhead: From Manchester, take Route 30/11 east toward the Bromley Ski Area. Look for the large trailhead parking lot on the left (north) side of Route 11 where the AT/LT crosses the road.

The Hike

There are two out-and-back approaches to Bromley, both on the AT/LT (white blazes). The approach from the south is 0.3 mile longer, but it has some interesting points along the way, namely Bromley Brook, a nice place to pause if you are hiking with a dog, and Bromley Shelter, where you can spend the night.

Hiking up Bromley Mountain feels easier than the distance might suggest. It is a good option if you are not quite up to either of the two nearby giants, Mount Equinox and Stratton Mountain, but still want a hike to an expansive view. Most of the route is in Green Mountain National Forest, but the summit lies in Hapgood State Forest, which is under long-term lease to the Bromley Ski Area.

From the trailhead, take the AT/LT–North, which begins as a dirt road at the east end of the elongated parking lot. After only 50 yards, turn left onto a footpath, crossing a stream via a curious steel girder placed there as a bridge.

The approach to the mountain is long and flat through an airy hardwood forest. At 0.5 mile the trail crosses Bromley Brook. There can be muddy sections over the next mile or so, but most of it is easily avoidable thanks to bog bridges (puncheons) or by rock hopping.

At 1.4 miles the trail begins to climb gently to a three-way intersection, which is really just the spur to Bromley Shelter and its outhouse. Go left (north) to reach the

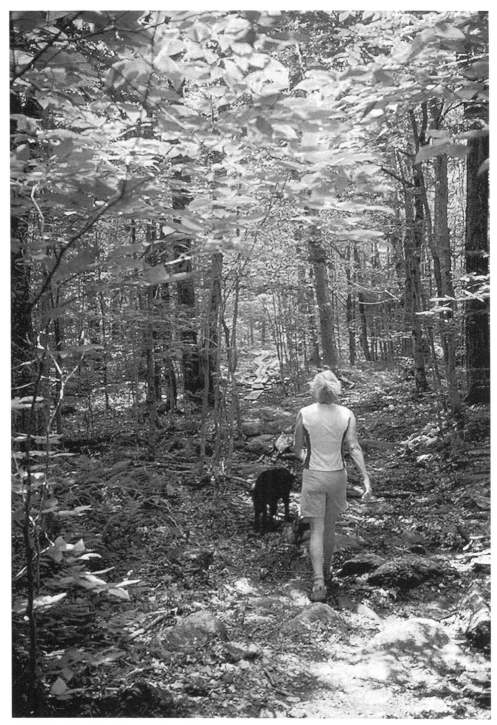

AT/LT to Bromley Mountain. LISA BALLARD

Bromley Mountain via the Appalachian Trail/Long Trail

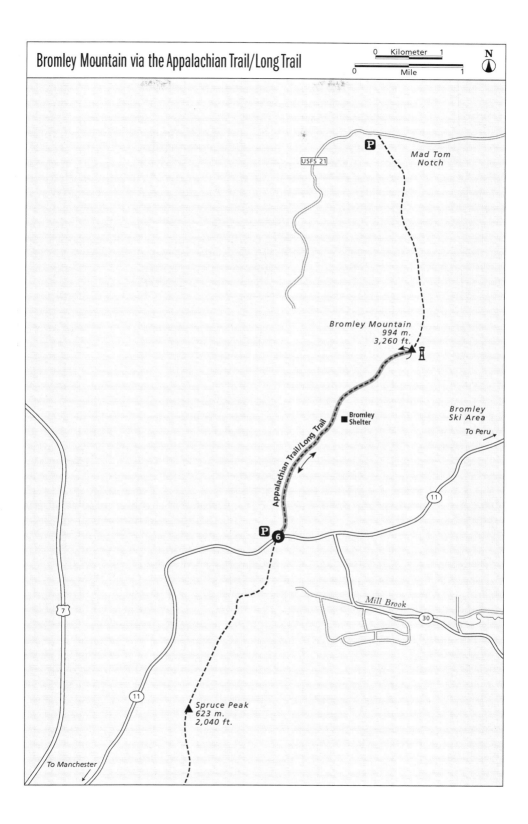

summit. Backpackers planning to sleep at Bromley Shelter should bear right (southeast) to drop their packs at the shelter before heading to the top. Bromley Shelter was rebuilt in 2003. It is a lean-to with a picnic table, composting privy, and sleeping "shelves" that span the width of the shelter.

Follow the AT/LT another 0.3 mile to a vista, then up through a fern forest. At 2.5 miles the trail breaks out onto the Run Around ski trail. Turn left, heading upward on the footpath through the center of the grassy ski trail.

The top of the mountain is an open meadow with more ski trails heading off in several directions. The old observation platform was taken down in 2012 because the wood was rotting. The Green Mountain Club (GMC) has funding and a design for a replacement, which is expected to be built in the early 2020s. It will, in GMC Manchester section president Marge Fish's words, "again be 40 feet tall, placed essentially in the same place, with an amazing 360-degree view." With or without the tower, the panorama in every direction, dominated by Stratton Mountain across the valley, is one of the best in southern Vermont.

Return by the same route.

Miles and Directions

0.0   Start at the trailhead for the AT/LT-North at the east end of the trailhead parking lot.

0.5   Cross Bromley Brook.

1.4   Turn left (north) at the three-way intersection near Bromley Shelter.

1.7   SCENIC VISTA!

2.5   Turn left (north) onto the Run Around ski trail.

2.8   SUMMIT! Return by the same route.

5.6   Arrive back at the trailhead.

A "GREEN" START

Hapgood State Forest was named after Marshall J. Hapgood, who is credited with the idea of establishing a federal forest reserve in Vermont, which ultimately became Green Mountain National Forest. Hapgood owned several mills that made wood products. He was an early proponent of selective logging to ensure regeneration of trees and to limit erosion at a time when clear-cutting without planned revegetation was the norm. In 1905 he offered to sell his land near Bromley Mountain, at a below-market price, to the Teddy Roosevelt administration. It took another twenty-seven years for the purchase to happen. This was the first tract of land that the US government acquired in Vermont for the purpose of conservation. Hapgood's initiative for the public to own and conserve Vermont's mountains and upland forests continues to benefit hikers today.

South-Central
Green Mountains

Danby to Killington

7 Baker Peak-Griffith Lake Loop

The perfect combo hike to both a scenic pond with waterfront tent sites and an open rock summit in the heart of the Big Branch Wilderness. Views north and south along the Otter Creek Valley.

General location: Danby
Distance: 8.6-mile lollipop
Hiking time: About 6.5 hours
Highest point: 2,850 feet
Elevation gain: 2,350 feet
Difficulty: Very strenuous as a day hike (due to mileage); moderate as an overnight backpacking trip
When to go: Year-round, except during mud season
Canine compatibility: Dog friendly

Trail surface: Dirt path
Land status: Public
Trail users: Hikers, snowshoers
Water availability: Pond
Map: USGS Danby quad
Special considerations: None
Trail contact: Green Mountain Club, (802) 244-7037, www.greenmountainclub.org; Green Mountain National Forest, Manchester District, (802) 362-2307, www.fs.usda.gov/gmfl

Finding the trailhead: From Danby, travel south on US 7 for 2 miles. Turn left (east) on South End Road, crossing railroad tracks, and go 0.4 mile to the trailhead and parking, which are on the left side of the road.

The Hike

Baker Peak is located in the middle of the 6,720-acre Big Branch Wilderness. While Griffith Lake is not inside the designated wilderness area, it is still a pristine backcountry destination. It is located in a narrow corridor between the Big Branch Wilderness and the Peru Peak Wilderness, where snowmobiling is allowed during the winter. Both early Native Americans and European settlers relied on the abundant natural resources of this region. Moose, black bear, whitetail deer, wild turkey, and beaver are common here.

Both Baker Peak and Griffith Lake make excellent hiking destinations alone, but the hike described here takes you to both in a day. The route is also perfect as an overnighter if you want to break up the mileage. You can camp at the Griffith Lake tent site, then either hike Baker Peak as a diversion or hike out over the peak. The route is described as a lollipop hike, a large loop that begins and ends on the same trail.

From the trailhead, follow the sign for the Griffith Lake Trail/Baker Peak Trail (blue blazes) into the hardwoods. The Griffith Lake Trail and the Baker Peak Trail are concurrent at first. The path is wide and smooth and climbs on an easy grade parallel to McGinn Brook, which is on your left. Sign in at the registration box and then bear left, dipping over a tributary of McGinn Brook and continuing along the opposite side of the brook.

Cascades on McGinn Brook. LISA BALLARD

At 0.5 mile the trail turns left uphill, where logs block an older route, then bends to the south like an elongated switchback, eventually returning to its generally easterly direction. Moments later, a sign marks the official border of the Big Branch Wilderness.

At about 1.1 miles a footbridge aids the traverse across a section of steep side-hill slab. After the bridge, the trail seems to hang on the hillside as it rounds a rocky outcropping.

At 1.5 miles look for a double blaze and a low rock cairn on your right, which signals a right turn onto a rougher, steeper path (no sign). Just after the turn, a short spur to a rock perch offers a nice view to the northwest. US 7 dissects the long, narrow valley below, which marks the rift between the Green Mountains and the Taconic Range. The Dorset marble quarry is to the south, and the village of Danby lies to the north.

From here the main trail swings up the side of a shallow ravine, where you can see the cascades of McGinn Brook below, through the trees. At the top of the ravine, the trail crosses the brook on slick moss-covered rocks. The Baker Peak Trail splits here to the left (north). Stay right on the Griffith Lake Trail, keeping the brook on your right, though the trail seems like a brook itself through this muddy area.

A short time later, the trail crosses a confluence of tributaries as they enter the main brook and then heads to drier ground. By 2.6 miles the streamlets peter out. The trail bends right, becoming a narrower path, and begins a long traverse to the southeast.

At 3.3 miles the Griffith Lake Trail meets the Appalachian Trail/Long Trail (AT/LT; white blazes) and runs concurrent with the AT/LT–South toward the lake. At 3.5 miles the trail reaches the lake, which is really a large pond with a beaver dam at its north end. The Green Mountain Club maintains the tent site on the east side of the lake and charges a small overnight fee (per person) for its use during the summer and fall. Camping is only permitted at designated spots.

To continue to Baker Peak from the lake, retrace your steps heading north on the AT/LT, returning to the junction with the Griffith Lake Trail at 3.7 miles. Stay on the AT/LT–North as it travels along a plateau through more hardwoods.

At 4.0 miles the trail dips down and zigzags through a boggy area over puncheons. At 4.3 miles the trail passes a large boulder as it descends gradually to another short bog bridge. From here the path begins to climb, gently at first, as it meanders through the woods in a northwesterly direction.

At 5.4 miles the AT/LT comes to a T at the Baker Peak Trail. Turn right, continuing north on the AT/LT, which is concurrent with the Baker Peak Trail to the summit of Baker Peak.

The last stretch is short and steep but an interesting scramble. The upper cone of Baker Peak is open rock, though it is not smooth. A metamorphic mountain, the entire summit area is a series of striated rock chunks, as if the peak were turned on its side and sliced off by some geologic force millions of years ago. It feels as though you are climbing up the back of a large, scaly dragon.

The trail reaches the top of Baker Peak at 5.6 miles. A marble quarry scars the ridge to the west. The views north and south along US 7 and the Otter Creek Valley can stretch for many miles on a clear day.

From the summit, retrace your steps back to the junction where the AT/LT and Baker Peak Trail meet, at 5.8 miles. This time, continue straight through the intersection, staying on the Baker Peak Trail (blue blazes). The descent is consistent on a moderate grade down the opposite side of the ravine from the AT/LT.

At 6.7 miles the Baker Peak Trail crosses a stream and then meets the Griffith Lake Trail, closing the loop. Bear right, continuing downhill, back around the elongated switchback.

Return to the trailhead at 8.6 miles.

Miles and Directions

0.0   Start at the trailhead for the Griffith Lake Trail/Baker Peak Trail.

0.5   Cross the boundary into the Big Branch Wilderness.

1.1   Cross a footbridge over steep sidehill slab.

1.5   Turn right, then pass a rock perch with a view of the valley.

1.9   The Griffith Lake Trail and Baker Peak Trail split. Bear right at the fork on the Griffith Lake Trail.

2.6   Bend right onto a narrower path and begin a long traverse to the southeast.

3.3   Head south at the junction with the AT/LT to reach the lake and the tent site.

3.5   LAKE! Return north on the AT/LT to continue to Baker Peak.

3.7   Bear right at the junction with the Griffith Lake Trail, continuing on the AT/LT-North.

4.0   Traverse a boggy area over extensive puncheons.

5.4   Turn right (north) at the T with the Baker Peak Trail. Scramble up rocks toward the summit. The Baker Peak Trail and AT/LT are concurrent here.

5.6   SUMMIT! Retrace the short distance to the junction of the Baker Peak Trail and the AT/LT.

5.8   Continue down the Baker Peak Trail when it splits from the AT/LT.

6.7   Close the loop at the junction with the Griffith Lake Trail. Turn right (west) onto the Griffith Lake Trail, heading back toward the trailhead.

8.6   Arrive back at the trailhead.

8 Okemo Mountain via the Healdville Trail

A pleasant hike through an airy hardwood forest along a cascading brook to a historic fire tower with a 360-degree view.

General location: Mount Holly
Distance: 5.8 miles out and back
Hiking time: About 4.5 hours
Highest point: 3,343 feet
Elevation gain: 1,943 feet
Difficulty: More challenging
When to go: Year-round
Canine compatibility: Dog friendly. Do not take your dog up the fire tower!
Trail surface: Well-maintained dirt path

Land status: Public
Trail users: Hikers, snowshoers, skiers
Water availability: Branch Brook at 1.5 miles
Map: USGS Mount Holly quad
Special considerations: None
Trail contact: Okemo State Forest, (802) 289-0603, www.fpr.vermont.gov/okemo-state-forest; Vermont Department of Forests, Parks and Recreation, (802) 886-2215, www.vtstate parks.com

Finding the trailhead: From the main entrance to the Okemo Mountain Resort in Ludlow, travel 4 miles north on Route 103. Turn left onto South Station Road. After crossing railroad tracks, look for the parking lot and trailhead on the left.

The Hike

The Green Mountain Club recommends staying off the Long Trail during mud season to protect it from excessive erosion, which makes Okemo Mountain, also called Ludlow Mountain, a particularly good choice if you have the urge to hike during the springtime before Memorial Day. The Healdville Trail (blue blazes), which is the main hiking trail up Okemo Mountain, is neither steep nor overly wet. It is located on the northern side of the mountain away from the ski area, so it feels like a true backcountry experience.

The origin of the name *Okemo* is unclear. Historians prefer the Chippewa translation, "chieftain," to the Abenaki translation, "louse." The origin of the name *Ludlow* is for a Viscount Ludlow, a wealthy English lord during the 1700s, or perhaps for his namesake town in Shropshire, where it means "hill by the rapid river." In the case of Ludlow Mountain, the Black River flows past its base, making "Ludlow" a fitting name for the mountain as well. Take your pick.

Though now maintained by the State of Vermont as part of the 7,327-acre Okemo State Forest, the Healdville Trail was originally built by the Vermont Youth Conservation Corps (VYCC). Formed in 1985, the VYCC hires young people, ages sixteen to twenty-four, to work on conservation projects throughout the state, such as building and maintaining hiking trails on state land.

The Healdville Trail is certainly well-maintained, with real footbridges rather than two old logs anchored in place. It starts over the first of these bridges before heading

Remains of the old fire-watcher's cabin on Okemo Mountain. LISA BALLARD

Okemo Mountain via the Healdville Trail

Healdville

103

Station Road

Healdville Road

To Ludlow

Branch Brook

P

8

Healdville Trail

OKEMO
STATE FOREST

LUDLOW MOUNTAIN

Okemo/
Ludlow Mountain

0   Kilometer   0.5
0   Mile   0.5

N

into a hardwood forest. The footing is easy, and the trail is wide. It quickly crosses another stream and then begins to climb steadily along the left side of Branch Brook. The brook tumbles over a number of small waterfalls, forming a series of tiny pools, each a perfect place to soak your feet.

At 1.5 miles the trail bends right and begins a long traverse to the south. At 1.9 miles it passes a sign that reads "Healdville Trail." The Catamount ski trail departs the Healdville Trail to the left (uphill) of the sign. Go straight, staying on the main trail.

The path dips down over a clear, rocky stream and then continues to climb. Just below the summit, it passes a stone chimney and the stone outline of the former fire-watcher's cabin, then comes to the intersection with a trail leading to the Mountain Road parking lot. Turn right to reach the fire tower at 2.9 miles.

Though slightly higher than the top of the ski area, the summit of Okemo is below tree line. However, the 55-foot fire tower lifts you into the sky above the tree-tops, permitting an impressive 360-degree view. Mount Washington and the White Mountains lie to the northeast. Mount Ascutney is closer and south of the Whites. Mount Monadnock is in the distance beyond the chairlift terminal. From the other side of the tower (opposite the ski area), you can see a significant part of the main ridge of the Green Mountains to the west.

Return by the same route.

Miles and Directions

0.0 Start at the trailhead for the Healdville Trail. Head into the hardwoods over a well-constructed footbridge.

1.5 Bend to the right and begin a long traverse to the south.

1.9 Pass the Healdville Trail sign, ignoring the smaller side trail.

2.7 Pass the remains of the former fire-watcher's cabin.

2.9 SUMMIT! Climb the fire tower for a 360-degree view, then return by the same route.

5.8 Arrive back at the trailhead.

⑨ Little Rock Pond and Green Mountain via the Homer Stone Brook Trail

A little bit of everything—a cascading brook, a large secluded pond, and mountain views—makes this a perfect day hike or an easy overnighter.

General location: South Wallingford
Distance: 7.1 miles out and back, including loop around pond
Hiking time: About 5 hours
Highest point: 2,509 feet
Elevation gain: 1,210 feet to Little Rock Pond, plus 660 feet to summit of Green Mountain
Difficulty: More challenging
When to go: Year-round, except during mud season
Canine compatibility: Dog friendly, though dogs should be on leash near ledges on Green Mountain and on the cliff above the pond. There is one rock that would be difficult for inexperienced dogs on the ascent up Green Mountain.
Trail surface: Dirt path with some rocky sections
Land status: Public
Trail users: Hikers, snowshoers
Water availability: Pond
Map: USGS Wallingford quad
Special considerations: None
Trail contact: Green Mountain Club, (802) 244-7037, www.greenmountainclub.org; Green Mountain National Forest, Rutland Office, (802) 747-6700, www.fs.usda.gov/gmfl

Finding the trailhead: In South Wallingford, turn east on Hartsboro Road, crossing over a small bridge and railroad tracks. At 0.1 mile, bear right (south) on Homer Stone Road. Go 0.3 mile to the trailhead on the left (east) side of the road. Park in the small grassy area by the trail sign.

The Hike

Most people (and other guidebooks) approach Little Rock Pond via the Appalachian Trail/Long Trail (AT/LT) from USFS Road 10 south of the pond. The Homer Stone Brook Trail (blue blazes) is 0.3 mile longer, round-trip, but it is a perfect 10 as far as hiking in southern Vermont goes. It begins with an easy walk through the woods that nips away at the elevation as it follows scenic Homer Stone Brook, paralleling the brook most of the way to the pond—a small lake really. Once at the pond, you can explore the loop around it, make the short climb up Green Mountain on its western shore, or both. The route described here takes you on the entire trek.

The Homer Stone Brook Trail begins as a smooth woods road, climbing easily up a hillside through a young hardwood forest. At about 0.2 mile the trail crosses the second of two stone walls, arriving at an unnamed junction with another woods road. Turn right, heading uphill.

At 0.3 mile bear right (south) at the fork, following the blue arrow, still climbing easily. The trail soon becomes more persistent as it heads upward through a stand of mature conifers and white birches.

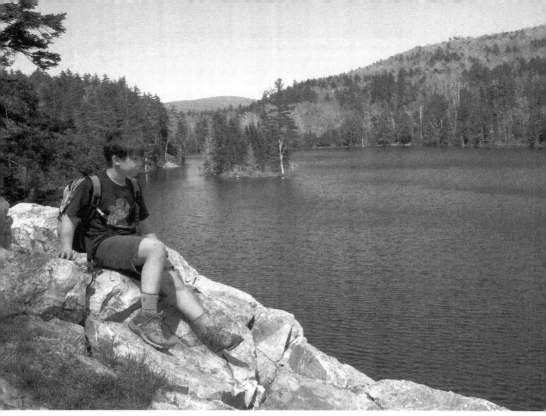

A boy resting on a cliff above Little Rock Pond. LISA BALLARD

At 0.6 mile you can hear Homer Stone Brook to your right. The trails levels off as it comes to a fork. Bear right (east), staying above the brook. Around the next bend, the brook is suddenly adjacent to the path on your right. Above this point, the ascent mellows, sometimes climbing next to the brook and sometimes high above it.

At 1.5 miles the trail levels off and comes to a junction with another woods road. Turn right (south), crossing the brook on stepping stones. (**Note:** This can be a wet crossing during spring runoff or after heavy rain.) The trail immediately forks on the opposite side of the stream. Bear right (west), go 30 yards, and then turn left (south) at the blue arrow. At the top of the short rise there is yet another junction. Turn left (east) and begin a steadier climb.

The trail remains wide but is now rockier and more eroded. It angles away from the brook on a noticeably steeper ascent until you reach Little Rock Pond and the end of the Homer Stone Brook Trail at 2.3 miles.

Turn right, following the western shoreline on the Green Mountain/Little Rock Pond Loop Trail (blue blazes), a narrower and lesser-used footpath than the AT/LT, which runs along the eastern shoreline. At about 2.4 miles the trail bends away from the pond to a junction where the mountain trail and the pond loop split. To climb Green Mountain, bear right (north) on the Green Mountain Trail.

The Green Mountain Trail winds uphill, then levels off on a shoulder of the mountain. It dips slightly on a short traverse to the south and then bends to the west, ascending steadily to the summit ridge. At about 2.9 miles the trail passes an interesting rib of rock protruding from the mountainside, as if a giant serpent were buried there and all that can be seen aboveground is its back.

Above the rock spine, the trail takes a sharp bend to the left (south). The trees turn coniferous, and the forest path gives way more and more to rock slab and ledge. After a short scramble up a 10-foot rock "wall" (follow the crack in the rock for the easiest route), the trail reaches the summit ridge. There are several rock perches en route to the true summit at 3.3 miles. For the best view, follow the pond view sign at the summit to a short spur across more open ledge. At the end of the spur, you can glimpse the southern end of the pond far below, though the panorama to the south is more impressive down the long Otter Creek Valley.

Retrace your steps down the Green Mountain Trail, arriving back at the pond at 4.2 miles. Turn right (south) at the pond, following the Little Rock Pond Loop. The loop passes over an impressive 40-foot cliff above the pond, where there are excellent views of the entire pond and its lone island.

At 4.5 miles the Little Rock Pond Loop ends at a T with the AT/LT (white blazes). Turn left and follow the AT/LT–North to close the loop around the pond. The trail immediately passes the Lula Tye tent site and the short spur trail that leads to an eight-person shelter. The shelter and tent site are maintained by the Green Mountain Club (GMC) and named for a woman who worked for the club for twenty-nine years during the first half of the twentieth century.

The AT/LT traverses the eastern shore of the pond. At 4.7 miles, at the opposite end of the pond, it passes a second tent site and a spur to the Little Rock Pond shelter, another eight-person shelter that is also maintained by the GMC. A caretaker oversees both shelters and tent sites during the summer, collecting a small usage fee from those who wish to camp there on a first-come, first-served basis.

At the Little Rock Pond tent site, the trail takes a sharp turn away from the pond to go around a small backwater, then arrives at the junction with the Green Mountain Trail. Bear left (west) on the Green Mountain Trail. The path immediately crosses a bridge over a beaver dam at the outlet to the pond, which is also the top (source) of Homer Stone Brook, closing the loop around the pond at 4.8 miles.

Retrace your steps back down the Homer Stone Brook Trail, returning to the trailhead at 7.1 miles.

Miles and Directions

0.0 Start at the trailhead for the Homer Stone Brook Trail.

0.2 Cross a stone wall at the four-way junction. Turn right, up the hill.

0.3 Bear right at the blue arrow, climbing through tall conifers and white birches.

0.6 Bear right at the fork. Come alongside Homer Stone Brook around the next bend in the trail.

1.5 Turn right, crossing the brook.

Little Rock Pond and Green Mountain
via the Homer Stone Brook Trail

0   Kilometer   1

0   Mile   1

N

Hartsboro Road

7

GREEN MOUNTAIN
NATIONAL FOREST

Appalachian Trail / Long Trail

Hartsboro Road

South
Wallingford

P
9

Homer Stone Brook Trail

Homer Stone Brook

Homer Stone Road

Little Rock Pond
Shelter

Green Mountain
765 m.
2,509 ft.

Little
Rock
Pond

Lula Tye
Shelter

Green Mountain Trail

Appalachian Trail / Long Trail

Otter Creek

7

2.3 POND! The Homer Stone Brook Trail ends at Little Rock Pond. Turn right on the Green Mountain/Little Rock Pond Loop Trail along the western shore of the pond.

2.4 Turn right on the Green Mountain Trail away from the pond.

2.9 Pass a rock spine. Climb rock slab and ledges to Green Mountain's summit ridge.

3.3 SUMMIT! Arrive at the summit of Green Mountain. Follow the short pond view spur for the best view of the pond and the Otter Creek Valley. Retrace your steps back to the pond.

4.2 Arrive back at the shoreline. Turn right on the Little Rock Pond Loop, continuing along the western shore of the pond and passing over a 40-foot cliff.

4.5 Turn left on the AT/LT–North, passing the Lula Tye tent site.

4.7 Pass the Little Rock Pond tent site. Turn sharply away from the pond to avoid a small backwater.

4.8 Cross a bridge over the beaver dam and pond outlet, closing the pond loop. Turn right on the Homer Stone Brook Trail and retrace your steps to the trailhead.

7.1 Arrive back at the trailhead.

TERMS OF THE TRAIL

There are a number of terms used to describe the trails and certain geologic features in the Green Mountains that might differ from other regions in the United States. Here's a list of the more common ones used in this book and their meanings:

Blaze: A trail marker, usually a rectangle painted vertically on a sturdy tree or rock.

Brook: Larger than a stream, but smaller than an official river. Brooks in Vermont are named corridors of water that resemble small rivers in size and water flow.

Lodge: A rustic mountain cabin maintained by the Green Mountain Club along the Long Trail, available to backpackers on a first-come, first-served basis. Also called a "camp."

Notch: A distinct narrow passage through the mountains, also called a "gap" or a "pass."

Puncheon: A narrow, low footbridge, usually two boards or two logs wide, that raises hikers just above the mud. Also called a "bog bridge" or "duck boards."

Ridge runner: A member of the Green Mountain Club, stationed atop a mountain with an alpine zone, who educates hikers on low-impact backcountry travel while monitoring the health of the fragile flora.

Spur: A short, unnamed side trail that ends at a specific destination, such as a cliff-top view or the side of a stream.

Stream: A corridor of water, usually unnamed, smaller than a brook. Many streams in the Green Mountains dry up by midsummer.

Streamlet: A small unreliable stream.

Woods road: A wide section of trail, for foot travel only, that was formerly a logging road or dirt road.

10 White Rocks Cliffs via the Keewaydin Trail

A relatively short hike to a dramatic cliff that passes a cascading waterfall on Bully Brook and some unusual rock cairns along the way.

General location: Wallingford
Distance: 3.2 miles out and back, including detour to Bully Brook
Hiking time: About 3 hours
Highest point: 2,400 feet
Elevation gain: 1,150 feet
Difficulty: Moderate
When to go: Year-round
Canine compatibility: Dog friendly. Dogs should be on leash around the picnic area at the trailhead and by the cliff.
Trail surface: Packed dirt, some rocks
Land status: Public

Trail users: Hikers, snowshoers
Water availability: Bully Brook
Map: USGS Wallingford quad
Special considerations: Before going on this hike, check with the Green Mountain National Forest office. The cliffs may be closed from early spring through mid-August if peregrine falcons are nesting here.
Trail contact: Green Mountain Club, (802) 244-7037, www.greenmountainclub.org; Green Mountain National Forest, Manchester District, (802) 362-2307, www.fs.usda.gov/gmfl

Finding the trailhead: From Route 140 between Wallingford and East Wallingford, turn southeast onto Sugar Hill Road. Take the first right onto White Rocks Picnic Road and park at the picnic area. The trailhead is at the far end of the parking lot by the USDA Forest Service notice board. (The trailhead for the White Rocks Ice Beds also leaves from this parking lot.) The picnic-area gate is open from 6 a.m. to 10 p.m. No overnight camping. *Note:* Though this hike can also be done entirely on the Appalachian Trail/Long Trail (AT/LT), which crosses Route 140 east of Sugar Hill Road, there is no trailhead parking. As Route 140 is narrow with many blind turns, this is not a recommended access point for this hike.

The Hike

From the parking lot, the Keewaydin Trail (blue blazes) seems more like a forest road than a footpath. It is wide and flat at first, but soon begins to ascend moderately and then rather steeply. The footing is smooth, which makes the climb easier as it angles up the hillside above Bully Brook.

At 0.2 mile a spur to the left gives a view of Bully Brook's cascades through the trees. The forest is healthy and lush around you. From here the trail becomes rockier and then crosses a stream just before joining the AT/LT at 0.4 mile.

To visit Bully Brook, turn left on the AT/LT–North (white blazes) and go a short way to a spur trail down to the cascades. To continue to the cliffs, turn right onto the AT/LT–South.

The trail becomes smooth again, climbing steeply through hardwoods. At 1.0 mile the spur to Greenwall Shelter departs to the left as the trail bends sharply right. It then meanders through the forest on a more moderate grade.

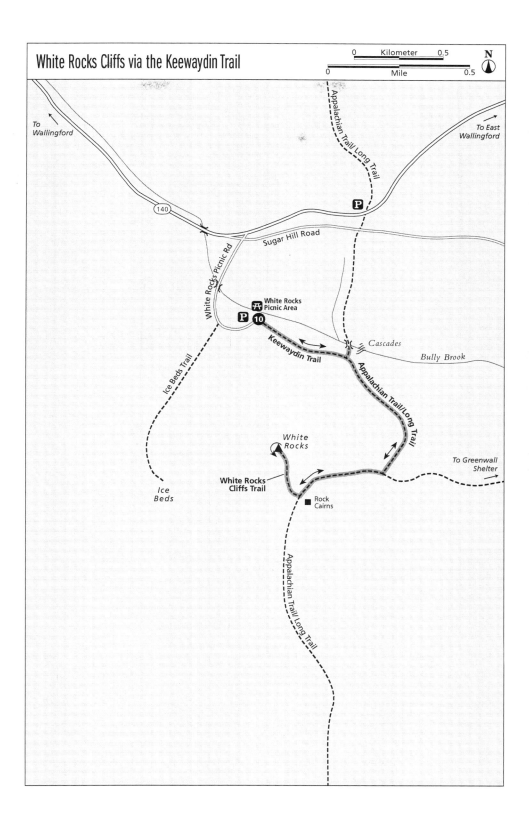

White Rocks Cliffs via the Keewaydin Trail

Kilometer
0   0.5

Mile
0   0.5

N

To Wallingford

To East Wallingford

Appalachian Trail/Long Trail

140

P

Sugar Hill Road

White Rocks Picnic Rd

White Rocks Picnic Area

P 10

Keewaydin Trail

Cascades

Bully Brook

Appalachian Trail/Long Trail

Ice Beds Trail

White Rocks

To Greenwall Shelter

White Rocks Cliffs Trail

Ice Beds

Rock Cairns

Appalachian Trail/Long Trail

View from the top of White Rock Cliffs. Lisa Ballard

At 1.4 miles the White Rocks Cliffs Trail (blue blazes) departs to the right. The junction is hard to miss. It is cluttered with small, odd rock formations reminiscent of Dr. Seuss. Various hikers have created this "cairn art" by stacking small rocks to look like mini-towers and other intriguing shapes. (A Forest Service employee dryly describes this rock cairn exhibit as "extensive.")

Turn right onto the White Rocks Cliffs Trail, which descends gently before coming to a clearing atop the cliff at 1.6 miles. The drop is almost 1,000 feet to the valley floor. If you head to the right through the scrubby trees, the view is eye-popping, including the Otter Creek Valley, the Taconic Range, and even the Adirondacks in New York.

Return by the same route.

Miles and Directions

0.0 Start at the trailhead for the Keewaydin Trail, a wide forest road.

0.4 Turn left at the junction with the AT/LT, heading north. Descend a short way to see Bully Brook, then return to the junction and follow the AT/LT-South.

1.0 Pass the spur to Greenwall Shelter. Stay on the AT/LT-South, which bends sharply to the right.

1.4 Turn right onto the White Rocks Cliffs Trail as you pass through cairn art.

1.6 CLIFF! Bear right through the brush and scrubby trees to get the best view, then return by the same route.

3.2 Arrive back at the trailhead.

11 White Rocks Ice Beds

A short hike to a mountainside boulder field that gives off cool air throughout the summer.

General location: Wallingford
Distance: 1.8 miles out and back
Hiking time: About 1.5 hours
Highest point: 1,400 feet
Elevation gain: 440 feet
Difficulty: Easy
When to go: Year-round
Canine compatibility: Not dog friendly due to vertical boulder field at destination

Trail surface: Packed earth, roots, slab, rocks, lots of boulder-scrambling
Land status: Public
Trail users: Hikers, snowshoers
Water availability: None
Map: USGS Wallingford quad
Special considerations: None
Trail contact: Green Mountain National Forest, Manchester District, (802) 362-2307, www.fs.usda.gov/gmfl

Finding the trailhead: From Route 140 between Wallingford and East Wallingford, turn southeast onto Sugar Hill Road. Take the first right onto White Rocks Picnic Road and park at the picnic area. The trailhead is on the right as you enter the parking lot. (The trailhead for White Rocks Cliffs also leaves from this parking lot.)

The Hike

Looking for a cool hike on a hot day? This one is cool both figuratively and literally. It goes to the base of an enormous boulder pile, which was likely formed during the last ice age. The rocks are Cheshire Quartzite, which gives them a white appearance. During the winter, ice accumulates within the deep, sheltered spaces between the boulders and lasts well into August.

From the parking lot, enter the woods on the Ice Beds Trail (blue blazes) over a couple of footbridges. The wide, rooted path immediately heads up over rocks and soon runs parallel to a cliff. It bends right behind a rocky outcropping that marks the edge of the cliff. Several spurs take you to the edge, though they are narrow and rough and can be treacherous. Have patience. At 0.3 mile the main trail reaches White Rocks Overlook, which offers an even better view of the peak and rockslide across the narrow ravine.

From here the footing alternates from smooth slab to scattered rocks and dirt. There is little undergrowth among the tall spruce trees, only moss, as you continue to parallel the cliff. At 0.5 mile the trail dips and then bends right, heading downhill, but take a few more steps straight ahead to another vista. This time the view extends across the hills to the west.

View from White Rocks Overlook. LISA BALLARD

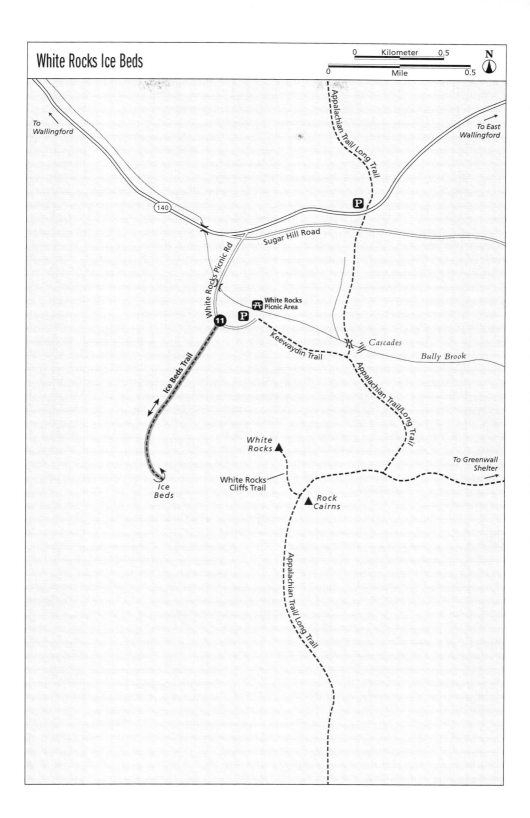

White Rocks Ice Beds

0   Kilometer   0.5

0   Mile   0.5

N

To Wallingford

To East Wallingford

Appalachian Trail/ Long Trail

140

Sugar Hill Road

White Rocks Picnic Rd

White Rocks Picnic Area

11

Ice Beds Trail

Keewaydin Trail

Cascades

Bully Brook

Appalachian Trail/Long Trail

Ice Beds

White Rocks

White Rocks Cliffs Trail

Rock Cairns

To Greenwall Shelter

Appalachian Trail/Long Trail

At the bottom of a short, steep hill, the trail bends left (west), traverses through the woods, and then continues downhill through a couple of short switchbacks until it levels off again. The footing is soft and smooth.

At 0.7 mile the trail reaches a fork. Bear left, heading downhill toward the brook, which you can hear but cannot see yet. A few yards later, the trail crosses a footbridge over the brook.

From here the trail levels off, heading east toward the cliffs. It crosses the narrow ravine that you saw from the lookouts above and begins to head gently uphill, reaching the ice beds at 0.9 mile. A cool draft flows continually down from the boulders. The streamlet, which emerges from the base of the boulders and is the result of runoff from melting ice, is a brisk 40 degrees.

Most people who visit the ice beds like to climb on the boulders. There are many rocky perches for a picnic on a hot day.

Return by the same route.

Miles and Directions

0.0 Start at the trailhead for the Ice Beds Trail.

0.3 Pass White Rocks Overlook and find a view of the mountaintop and the enormous rockslide.

0.5 VISTA! The trail bends sharply to the right and heads downhill.

0.7 Bear left at the fork, heading downhill toward a brook.

0.9 ICE BEDS! Climb the boulders to find the perfect lunch spot, then return by the same route.

1.8 Arrive back at the trailhead.

12 Killington Peak via the Bucklin Trail

Hike to the alpine summit of the second-highest peak in Vermont. Numerous wildflowers in early summer; optional overnight at Cooper Lodge (cabin); spectacular view, particularly to the north along the spine of the Green Mountains.

General location: Mendon
Distance: 7.6 miles out and back
Hiking time: About 6 hours
Highest point: 4,235 feet
Elevation gain: 2,480 feet
Difficulty: Very strenuous (due to elevation gain)
When to go: Year-round, except during mud season
Canine compatibility: Dog friendly. The GMC Killington section advises that local vets have reported a sharp increase in dogs getting quilled by porcupines on this route. Keeping your dog on leash may be prudent.

Trail surface: Packed and smooth dirt trail most of the way; steep, rocky scramble above Cooper Lodge
Land status: Public
Nearest amenities: Killington or Rutland
Trail users: Hikers, snowshoers, skiers
Water availability: Brook, spring at Cooper Lodge
Map: USGS Killington Peak quad
Special considerations: None
Trail contact: Green Mountain Club, (802) 244-7037, www.greenmountainclub.org

Finding the trailhead: From Rutland, take US 4 east for 5 miles. Turn right (south) on Wheelerville Road (dirt). From the split of US 4 and Route 100 in Killington, follow US 4 west for 4.7 miles to Wheelerville Road on the left (south). Follow Wheelerville Road for 4 miles, passing the Rutland Watershed Area on your left. Just before a 90-degree bend in the road (known as Brewers Corners), look for the trailhead on the left.

The Hike

Killington Peak is the highest of the six peaks that make up the Killington ski resort and one of only five summits with elevations over 4,000 feet in Vermont. There are four ways to climb this towering peak, from the north and from the south along the Appalachian Trail/Long Trail (AT/LT), from the east up one of the ski area's interpretive hiking trails, and from the west via the Bucklin Trail.

The Bucklin Trail is the shortest route up Killington Peak and a truer backcountry experience than routes on the ski area side. It sustained heavy damage as a result of Tropical Storm Irene in 2011. Irene, which dropped 11 inches of rain in some areas of Vermont, hit the area around Killington particularly hard. One neighboring town, Pittsfield, was completely isolated for weeks because all of the surrounding roads were washed out. In 2012 the Green Mountain Club (GMC) rerouted sections of the Bucklin Trail and repaired or rebuilt all of the bridges along the route.

Cooper Lodge en route to Killington Peak. MARK AIKEN

From the trailhead, the Bucklin Trail (blue blazes) enters the woods on an old woods road that is also part of the Catamount Trail, a winter-use trail for Nordic skiing and snowshoeing. The Catamount Trail system winds 300 miles through the state and is marked with small blue plastic diamonds. Ignore them and instead follow the blue painted rectangles, the universal blaze for an access trail to the AT/LT. (The AT/LT is marked with white rectangles.)

The Bucklin Trail passes a kiosk at 0.3 mile and crosses Brewers Brook over a footbridge. It then follows the brook, gradually rising away from it as the Catamount Trail veers off to the left. The Bucklin Trail narrows to a footpath through a plethora of wildflowers in early summer, including clover, daisy, buttercup, wild rose, and devil's paintbrush. The trail rolls up and down and over several sections of puncheons and wooden steps.

At 1.5 miles the trail recrosses Brewers Brook on a substantial bridge and then over a smaller bridge across a side stream. It continues up the other side of the brook, again distancing itself from the water. At 2.2 miles look across Brewers Brook to the opposite bank, where Irene Falls cascades a hundred feet to the brook.

At 3.0 miles the Bucklin Trail comes to a junction with an unnamed route used for evacuating injured backcountry skiers during the winter. The evacuation route is blocked by a low dirt berm. Bear right, heading uphill. Until this point, the ascent is gentle, and the trail is smooth and flat. Here the trail becomes steeper, though the

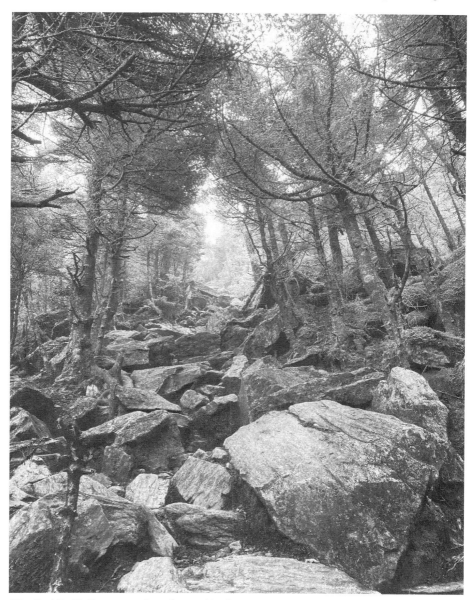

The Bucklin Trail starts gently and smoothly then turns steep and rocky! MARK AIKEN

footing remains smooth. When a ridgeline first appears through the treetops, look for an unusual twisted tree next to the trail. It is about 3 feet in diameter and has a huge hollow in its uphill side that is big enough to stand in.

The trail flattens out briefly as you enter the subalpine zone, where coniferous trees take over. At 3.5 miles the Bucklin Trail reaches the AT/LT. Continue uphill on the AT/LT–South. From here on, more roots crisscross the trail, though the ascent eases.

At the next fork, a sign points to a water source on the right, but turn left to reach Cooper Lodge at 3.6 miles. Cooper Lodge is the highest elevated of the many cabins maintained by the Green Mountain Club along the Long Trail. Constructed of stone and wood, the lodge is relatively spacious, with sleeping platforms that hold up to sixteen people and a full-size picnic table inside it. The entire northwestern side of the cabin has windows, although the view is mostly obstructed by trees.

Cooper Lodge was built in 1939 by the Vermont Forest Service. It is located on state land that was donated by Mortimer R. Proctor, a former president of the GMC and governor of Vermont. Proctor made the donation in honor of Charles P. Cooper, another former president of the club. The GMC is considering removal of this shelter, which is the object of frequent vandalism and abuse due to its easy access from the ski area, so backpackers should check with the club first before assuming they will find shelter there. A GMC ridge runner may collect a small, per-person fee for overnight use of the lodge. If Cooper Lodge is full, bear right, up the log steps, to find a number of tent platforms in the woods just above the cabin.

From here the climb to the summit is short but utterly steep and rocky. The rocks feel like steps prepared for giants rather than humans.

At 3.8 miles the trail arrives at the summit. While not expansive, it is bare and well worth the climb, particularly for the view to the north, where you can see Mount Mansfield along the spine of Vermont's highest peaks. Blue Ridge Mountain lies to the left of Pico Peak by Chittenden Reservoir. Tree-covered Little Killington lies to the west in the foreground, with Bald Mountain and the Rutland Valley farther away. On a clear day, look through the gap on the far side of Rutland to see the Adirondacks. To catch Mount Ascutney to the southeast, you have to look through the jumble of communication equipment on an old fire tower, which is not open to the public.

The rocky trail beyond the summit leads to the Killington gondola only 200 yards away. On weekends, many people ride up the gondola and then make the short hike from there to the summit. It is best to save this trek for midweek if you want this popular peak to yourself.

Return by the same route.

Miles and Directions

0.0 Start at the trailhead for the Bucklin Trail, concurrent with the Catamount Trail.
0.3 Cross Brewers Brook on a footbridge.
1.5 Recross Brewers Brook on another bridge.
2.2 IRENE FALLS! Continue on the Bucklin Trail.
3.0 Junction with a backcountry-skiing evacuation trail. Turn right, heading uphill.
3.5 Junction with the AT/LT. Take the AT/LT–South to reach Killington Peak.
3.6 COOPER LODGE! Continue to the summit, up steep rocks.
3.8 SUMMIT! Return by the same route.
7.6 Arrive back at the trailhead.

13 Pico Peak via the Sherburne Pass Trail

A steady climb that passes a cave and ascends through two climate zones—northern hardwood forest and boreal forest—to a small hut with a huge view to the north and south.

General location: Killington
Distance: 5.8 miles out and back
Hiking time: About 4.5 hours
Highest point: 3,957 feet
Elevation gain: 1,807 feet
Difficulty: More challenging
When to go: Year-round, except during mud season
Canine compatibility: Dog friendly
Trail surface: Dirt path, rocks, gravel

Land status: Public
Trail users: Hikers, snowshoers
Water availability: Unreliable
Map: USGS Pico Peak quad
Special considerations: None
Trail contact: Green Mountain Club, (802) 244-7037, www.greenmountainclub.org; Green Mountain National Forest, Rochester District, (802) 767-4261, www.fs.usda.gov/gmfl

Finding the trailhead: From Rutland, take US 4 west for 9 miles to the top of Sherburne Pass, just west of the entrance to the Pico Peak Ski Area. The trailhead begins at the end of the parking lot on the south side of the road, across the street from the Inn at Long Trail. If approaching from the east, from the junction where US 4 and Route 100 North split near the main entrance to Killington Resort, continue 1.6 miles west on US 4 to the top of Sherburne Pass.

The Hike

The Sherburne Pass Trail (blue blazes) was originally a section of the Appalachian Trail/Long Trail (AT/LT) and dates back to 1913, when the Long Trail was first cut. In the 1990s the AT/LT was relocated slightly west of the Sherburne Pass Trail to allow for a potential ski area expansion. The expansion did not happen, but the relocation of the AT/LT remains, which is a good thing if your goal is to hike to the top of Pico Peak. While still a popular hike, you won't see any through-hikers these days.

From the sign-in box, the Sherburne Pass Trail starts climbing moderately through a hardwood forest. A fertile mix of ferns, low leafy shrubs, wood sorrel, and grasses grow along the edges of this well-worn trail. The footing varies from rocks and roots to sections of slab. Ignore the first unmarked but obvious spur to the right. It leads to a ski area work road with no view.

At 1.3 miles the trail passes two sinkholes on the right. The first is smaller, about 7 feet deep. The second is twice that size, with two short unofficial footpaths leading into it. A stream also flows into the larger hole, disappearing into the earth. Avoid exploring the sinkholes. The soil can be unstable around them, and both are part of a small cave, which is unsafe for novice spelunking.

Above the sinkholes the trail climbs gradually, crossing a small streamlet, and then turns toward the west, gaining noticeable elevation. Eventually, it swings back to the south as the trees become predominantly evergreen. It turns to the west again, then continues on a long, shallow ascent to a junction with the Summit Glades ski trail (no sign). From the ski trail, you get a lengthy view to the north past Deer Leap Overlook and the Chittenden Reservoir and on to some of the higher peaks in the Green Mountain chain.

After 20 paces, the Sherburne Pass Trail reenters the woods on the left, marked by only a blue blaze (no sign). At this point, you have two choices: take the steeper ski trail or the flatter footpath to the summit. Opting for the footpath, turn left and then continue along the now-flat trail. Just after a small spring, marked by a white pipe poking out of the hillside, the trail reaches Pico Shelter, also called Pico Camp, at 2.5 miles.

Pico Shelter is an excellent place to sleep if you are backpacking. It has rough bunks, a table, and a nice view of Killington Peak. The shelter is available on a first-come, first-served basis. A ridge runner from the Green Mountain Club stays here and may collect the small overnight fee. If the shelter is full, you may not tent-camp by the shelter. The overflow camping area is 0.3 mile away on a nearby ski trail. *Note:* Campfires are not allowed in the Coolidge Range (Killington and Pico region).

For the final climb to the summit, turn right, passing the entrance to the shelter, onto the Pico Link Trail (blue blazes). The trail climbs steeply past the back of the shelter to another ski trail. At the junction with the ski trail, look left for a more expansive view of Killington Peak.

Cross the ski trail and reenter the woods by a small rock cairn. The trail continues to climb steeply to a gravel work road. Turn left, heading up the road for a few paces, and then right through a strip of trees onto yet another ski trail, called Forty-Niner (no sign). Turn left, continuing uphill on Forty-Niner toward the communication towers on the summit.

Just below the summit, at 2.8 miles, the trail comes to the Warming Hut and the top of a chairlift. The Warming Hut is open year-round. In the winter, it serves skiers as a first-aid and information cabin. In the summer, it is empty. The small deck on the front of the hut is a perfect picnic spot, with built-in benches around its railing. The views of nearby Killington to the south and Ascutney, the pointed peak with ski trails farther to the southeast, are spectacular. Looking past the lift terminal to the north, the layers of peaks include Mount Abraham, Mount Ellen, and even Mount Mansfield on a clear day.

For a view to the west, you need to hike slightly farther to the true summit of the mountain at 2.9 miles. However, the summit is a jumble of work roads, maintenance buildings, lift terminals, and communication towers. It is worth a quick glance, but the Warming Hut offers the serenity that most hikers seek on a mountaintop. *Note:* Always stay clear of the chairlifts, as the lifts can turn any time, even in summer.

Return by the same route.

Pico Peak via the Sherburne Pass Trail

Miles and Directions

0.0   Start at the trailhead for the Sherburne Pass Trail. Climb moderately through a lush hardwood forest.

1.3   Pass two sinkholes beside the trail.

2.5   PICO SHELTER! Turn right onto the Pico Link Trail, heading uphill.

2.8   Have a picnic and take in the views to the north, east, and south at the Warming Hut.

2.9   SUMMIT! Best spot for a view to the west. Return by the same route.

5.8   Arrive back at the trailhead.

◀ *The view from the upper trail on Pico Peak.* LISA BALLARD

14 Deer Leap Overlook

Short hike to a dramatic cliff with a 180-degree view of Pico Peak and the surrounding countryside.

General location: Killington
Distance: 2.2 miles out and back
Hiking time: About 2 hours
Highest point: 2,670 feet
Elevation gain: 520 feet
Difficulty: Moderate
When to go: Year-round, except during mud season
Canine compatibility: Dog friendly, but a busy trail without water. Dogs should be on leash around other people and at the summit cliff.

Trail surface: Dirt path, mud, puncheon sections
Land status: Public
Trail users: Hikers, rock climbers, snowshoers
Water availability: None
Map: USGS Pico Peak quad
Special considerations: None
Trail contact: Green Mountain Club, (802) 244-7037, www.greenmountainclub.org; Green Mountain National Forest, Rutland Office, (802) 747-6700, www.fs.usda.gov/gmfl

Finding the trailhead: From the junction of US 7 and US 4 in Rutland, travel 9 miles east on US 4, just west of the entrance to the Pico Peak Ski Area. Park in the large dirt lot on the south side of the road. Carefully cross the road to the trailhead, which leaves from the right (east) side of the Inn at Long Trail. If approaching from the east, from the junction where US 4 and Route 100 North split near the main entrance to the Killington Resort, continue 1.6 miles west on US 4 to the top of Sherburne Pass.

The Hike

Deer Leap Overlook, also known as Deer Leap Cliff and Deer Leap Lookout, is a cliffy shoulder of Deer Leap Mountain. It is a popular perch with a stunning view of Pico Peak directly across Sherburne Pass. It towers above US 4, gleaming bright white from the high amount of quartz in the granite. The hike passes just east of "Maine Junction," the point where after 105 miles together, the Appalachian Trail (AT) and Long Trail (LT) split, with the AT turning east toward New Hampshire and the LT continuing north toward Canada.

At the trailhead, sign in at the box, then follow the Sherburne Pass Trail (blue blazes) into the woods. At first, the well-used trail climbs moderately, heading east parallel to US 4, away from your cliff-top destination. The trail is initially rocky and rough.

At about 0.2 mile the trail dips downhill and then levels off. The footing becomes smoother.

At 0.3 mile the trail bends away from the road, climbing steadily. Be careful to stay on the trail and off the unofficial shortcuts in this section to help reduce human impact.

At 0.5 mile the trail bends to the right (east) and ends abruptly at the Appalachian Trail. Turn left onto the AT South (white blazes), though you are actually heading north briefly.

About 200 feet later, the AT comes to the junction with the Deer Leap Overlook Trail (blue blazes). Turn left (northwest) onto the Deer Leap Overlook Trail. The climb is steady at first, then becomes steeper until it crests a short ridge. Here the flora changes abruptly to white birches and evergreens. The trail levels off and then descends slightly as it crosses the ridge.

The path traverses a muddy area over several puncheons and then reaches the junction with the spur to Deer Leap Overlook at 0.9 mile. Bear left at this junction, taking the higher path to stay on the ridge.

Deer Leap Overlook LISA BALLARD

At 1.1 miles the trail dips sharply, then winds downhill briefly over a narrow boardwalk to the lookout. The open rock knob is a perfect spot for a picnic. Pico Peak dominates the view to the south, though you can also see the hills to the east and west.

Return by the same route.

Miles and Directions

0.0 Start at the trailhead for the Sherburne Pass Trail. Head east, parallel to US 4.

0.3 Bend left, away from US 4, climbing steadily.

0.5 Turn left onto the AT South. After 200 feet, turn left (northwest) onto the Deer Leap Overlook Trail.

0.9 Bear left onto the spur trail to Deer Leap Overlook. Dip down and then cross the narrow boardwalk.

1.1 OVERLOOK! Return to the trailhead by the same route.

2.2 Arrive back at the trailhead.

15 Blue Ridge Mountain

A mid-distance hike past a waterfall and through beautiful forest to a rewarding lookout.

General location: Mendon
Distance: 4.8 miles out and back
Hiking time: About 4 hours
Highest point: 3,278 feet
Elevation gain: 1,490 feet
Difficulty: Moderate
When to go: Year-round, except during mud season
Canine compatibility: Dog friendly
Trail surface: Packed dirt, loose gravel, rocky sections

Land status: Public
Nearest amenities: Rutland or Killington
Trail users: Hikers, snowshoers
Water availability: Stream beside trail
Map: USGS Chittenden quad
Special considerations: None
Trail contact: Green Mountain Club, (802) 244-7037, www.greenmountainclub.org; Green Mountain National Forest, Rutland Office, (802) 747-6700, www.fs.usda.gov/gmfl

Finding the trailhead: From the junction of US 7 and US 4 in Rutland, follow US 4 east for 6 miles. Turn left (north) on Old Turnpike Road and go 1 mile. The trailhead is a pullout on the left (west) side of the road.

The Hike

Blue Ridge Mountain remains largely under the radar for most nonlocals because, although the Appalachian Trail/Long Trail passes just miles away, it is not part of Vermont's famous wilderness end-to-end footpath. Blue Ridge is a good-sized mountain and a satisfying hike, partly because it is pleasantly untrafficked.

The Canty Trail (blue blazes) is named for landowners through whose property the trail formerly traveled. The trail was rerouted onto Green Mountain National Forest land in 2014. A sign at the old trailhead directs hikers to the new access point.

From the trailhead on Old Turnpike Road, immediately descend for 0.2 mile to the first of several stream crossings. The trail traverses a boggy area over sections of puncheons that are surrounded by waves of white trillium in the spring.

At 0.4 mile the trail leaves a stand of quiet hemlocks and climbs a wooded ridgeline that falls steeply off both sides. After leaving the ridge, ignore several unofficial trails before two more stream crossings, the second of which ascends stone stairs on the far bank.

At 0.8 mile the trail joins a logging road for a short distance before splitting right, bringing you to your first significant ascent alongside Sawyer Brook. The trail is wide here and dotted with round rocks and stones. It ascends steadily until coming to a flat spot in the midst of a circle of large maple trees at 1.3 miles. The trail then veers left and continues climbing diagonally across the flank of Blue Ridge Mountain.

Cascading waterfall midway up the Canty Trail on Blue Ridge Mountain. MARK AIKEN

At 1.6 miles, still in the middle of the diagonal ascent, a spur trail leads downhill to the right (southeast) to a beautiful cascading waterfall. The cascade runs even in the dry season and can be a refreshing cool-off spot on a summer day.

The trail continues its diagonal ascent, with the babbling brook audible below, until it meets the brook head-on. It then turns sharply left away from the brook and toward the summit. The pitch mellows somewhat as it continues upward.

At 1.9 miles the character of the forest shifts. Maples and ashes give way to rugged, peeling birches and firs. Slightly beyond, you sense the approaching summit as you gain the shoulder of the mountain and continue the gentle climb. The trees become shorter and more stunted until you arrive at a Y at 2.3 miles. The fork to the right leads to the viewless, wooded summit 20 steps away. Go to the summit for bragging rights. For a view, follow the left spur, which leads to Rutland Lookout at 2.4 miles, a lofty perch whose view includes the ski trails and top ski lift on Pico Peak to the southeast and the Coolidge Range stretching southwest to Mount Equinox. On a clear day, you can see New York's Taconics and Adirondacks. The city of Rutland sits in the valley below.

Return by the same route.

Miles and Directions

0.0 Start at the trailhead for the Canty Trail.

0.4 Traverse a wooded ridgeline.

1.6 WATERFALL! Take the short spur trail to the waterfall.

2.3 SUMMIT! Bear right at the fork to the treed summit, then return to the fork and head left for a view.

2.4 RUTLAND LOOKOUT! Return by the same route.

4.8 Arrive back at the trailhead.

North-Central Green Mountains

Brandon Gap to Huntington

16 Mount Horrid's Great Cliff

A short, steep hike to a cliff-top perch that rewards with long views east and west into the neighboring states of New Hampshire and New York.

General location: Goshen
Distance: 1.4 miles out and back
Hiking time: About 1.5 hours
Highest point: 2,800 feet
Elevation gain: 620 feet
Difficulty: Moderate
When to go: Year-round, except during mud season
Canine compatibility: Dog friendly
Trail surface: Packed dirt, rocks

Land status: Public
Trail users: Hikers, snowshoers
Water availability: None
Map: USGS Mount Carmel quad
Special considerations: Cliff area may be closed if peregrine falcons are nesting there.
Trail contact: Green Mountain Club, (802) 244-7037, www.greenmountainclub.org; Green Mountain National Forest, Rochester District, (802) 767-4261, www.fs.usda.gov/gmfl

Finding the trailhead: From the junction of Routes 100 and 73 in Rochester, head west on Route 73 for 9.3 miles. The trailhead parking is on the south side of the road just after the top of Brandon Gap. Cross the road to find the trailhead for the Long Trail (LT)-North. From the junction of US 7 and Route 73 in Brandon, head east on Route 73 for 8.2 miles. The trailhead is just before the top of Brandon Gap when approaching from this side.

The Hike

The exposed rock on Mount Horrid's Great Cliff dates back to the earliest geologic times. Though not the summit of Mount Horrid, it is truly a great cliff, towering 800 feet above Route 73 and making up the northern wall of Brandon Gap.

Although the route to the Great Cliff is via the Long Trail (LT)–North (white blazes), the trail actually heads east at first, parallel to Route 73, and then bends north into the woods at a large sign containing historical information on the LT. It is a smooth, steep climb up a boulder-strewn hillside.

At about 0.2 mile the path passes a sign marking the boundary of the 24,237-acre Breadloaf Wilderness, the largest designated wilderness within Green Mountain National Forest. The Breadloaf Wilderness was created in 1984 and is named for Breadloaf Mountain, which is farther north along the LT and the highest point within the wilderness area.

The trail continues to wind upward. At 0.3 mile it mellows somewhat, though it still climbs steeply at times, quickly rising above Brandon Gap. The trail passes through stands of birches and maples, making this a colorful route during peak fall foliage.

At 0.5 mile the ascent is aided by stone steps. The cliff becomes apparent on your right as the trail bends east. It levels off briefly, crossing some slab, where you can glimpse the opposite side of the gap through the leaves.

0 Kilometer 0.5

0 Mile 0.5

N

Cape Lookoff
Mountain
1,024 m.
3,360 ft.

Long Trail

Mount Horrid
980 m.
3,216 ft.

BREADLOAF
WILDERNESS
AREA

The Great
Cliff

To Goshen,
Brandon

73

To
Rochester

16

P

Long Trail

A short way later, the climb becomes steeper again and rockier, with longer stone staircases. At 0.6 mile the steps peter out at the spur to the Great Cliff, which departs to the right (east; blue blazes). *Note:* Mount Horrid's Great Cliff is a known nesting site for peregrine falcons, typically between March and July. If falcons are nesting, the cliff area might be closed to hikers.

The short spur trail to the cliff continues to climb steadily, though less steeply at first. It levels off completely as it approaches the cliff at 0.7 mile. From this rocky outcropping, 800 feet above the road, the views extend to the Adirondacks in New York and the White Mountains in New Hampshire on a clear day.

Return by the same route.

The view west from Mount Horrid's Great Cliff. LISA BALLARD

Miles and Directions

0.0 Start at the trailhead for the LT–North.

0.2 Cross the boundary into the Breadloaf Wilderness.

0.5 Stone steps aid the ascent.

0.6 Bear right (east) onto the spur trail to the Great Cliff.

0.7 CLIFF! Return by the same route.

1.4 Arrive back at the trailhead.

17 Silver Lake

A pristine lake with a number of tent sites and an interpretive trail with numbered historical points around its perimeter.

General location: Goshen
Distance: 5.1-mile lollipop
Hiking time: About 3.5 hours
Highest point: 1,250 feet
Elevation gain: 630 feet
Difficulty: Moderate
When to go: Year-round
Canine compatibility: Dog friendly. Pets must be on a leash around the picnic area and the campground.
Trail surface: Gravel road, packed dirt

Land status: Public
Trail users: Hikers, mountain bikers, snowshoers
Water availability: Water source at campground
Map: USGS East Middlebury quad
Special considerations: None
Trail contact: Moosalamoo Association, (802) 989-6980, www.moosalamoo.org; Green Mountain National Forest, Rochester District, (802) 767-4261, www.fs.usda.gov/gmfl

Finding the trailhead: On the east side of Lake Dunmore, follow Route 53 for 0.2 mile south of Branbury State Park. Park at the trailhead. If full, there are three or four spots in front of boulder barricades along Route 53 between the parking lot and the state park.

The Hike

This hike is over 5 miles long but gets a moderate rating because the elevation gain is minimal. The approach to Silver Lake is the same as the hike to Mount Moosalamoo for the first half mile. After that, it is an entirely different hiking experience, to a pristine lake rather than a mountaintop.

From the trailhead parking area, walk up a short rise to a Forest Service access road, an unpaved lane that is not opened to motorized traffic. Turn right and head up the road, which soon passes under a huge pipe, called a penstock. The penstock feeds water from Silver Lake above to a small hydroelectric power station on Route 53 below. It was built in 1922 to provide power to the iron mines in Mineville, New York, on the other side of Lake Champlain. Today, it produces electricity for over 800 homes in the Moosalamoo area. This industrial intrusion is completely hidden from hikers except for the penstock.

At 0.5 mile the road passes the top of the Falls of Lana, an impressive waterfall fed by Sucker Brook, which is often a raging torrent. Use care if you hike down toward the falls for a better look, as the roots are slick from constant spray.

From the top of the falls, the trail parallels Sucker Brook as it climbs gently to the junction with the trail to Rattlesnake Cliffs, aka Rattlesnake Point, and the summit of Mount Moosalamoo. The junction is also notable for the public outhouse in the middle of it. Turn right, continuing along the service road.

A view of Mount Moosalamoo across Silver Lake. LISA BALLARD

As you climb toward the pond, ignore the various side trails and roads that enter periodically from the right, including a significant fork at 1.1 miles.

At 1.3 miles the road passes a campground operated by Green Mountain National Forest. It is manned during the summer months by a host for the campground. Beyond the campground, the route reaches a grassy area at the northern tip of Silver Lake, where it meets the Rocky Point Interpretive Trail (blue blazes), the trail around the lake.

The 2.5-mile interpretive trail has eighteen signed points of interest. Head right, over the small dam. The dam did not create Silver Lake; it merely enlarged it. The original lake was about 6 feet lower. It has been a backcountry destination since the mid-1800s. In its prime, from 1880 to 1910, the Silver Lake Hotel stood where the picnic area is today and entertained up to a hundred guests at a time. Now, only a few foundation stones remain.

Once past the dam, the loop around the lake becomes increasingly primitive, but it is well-marked and well-maintained. At about 1.9 miles the Chandler Ridge Trail enters from the right. The Chandler family lived at Silver Lake for about sixty years starting in the 1870s. During that time, members of the family uncovered various tools and arrowheads left by the Abenakis. These artifacts eventually led archaeologists to find two dugout canoes at the bottom of the lake, both over 600 years old.

At 2.1 miles the trail climbs over a small cave in the rocks. Then, as you round the swampier southern end of the lake, Mount Moosalamoo dominates the view across the water.

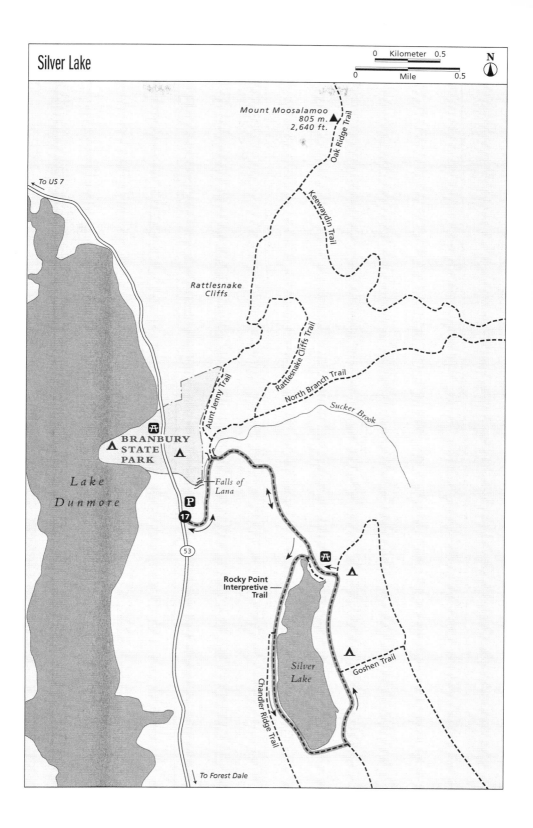

Silver Lake

0 Kilometer 0.5
0 Mile 0.5

N

Mount Moosalamoo
805 m.
2,640 ft.

Oak Ridge Trail

Keewaydin Trail

To US 7

Rattlesnake Cliffs

Rattlesnake Cliffs Trail

North Branch Trail

Aunt Jenny Trail

Sucker Brook

BRANBURY
STATE
PARK

Lake Dunmore

Falls of Lana

P

17

53

Rocky Point Interpretive Trail

Chandler Ridge Trail

Silver Lake

Goshen Trail

To Forest Dale

The footing becomes drier and smoother on the second half of the lake loop. At one point, the trail passes a glade of birches leading to a piney point. The area is open under the canopy and would be a perfect place to camp if it were allowed. Overnight camping, however, is only permitted at designated campsites, closer to the service road.

From here the trail dips away from the lake, crosses a stream, and then rises to an intersection with the Leicester Hollow Trail at 2.8 miles, which is more forest road than footpath. A little farther, the Goshen Trail enters from the right. The path is now wide, and the footing is easy.

At about 3.1 miles the path passes fifteen campsites that are reserved for tent camping, with picnic tables and fire pits. Check out the old-fashioned hand-pumped drinking fountain on the left. There is a nominal fee for camping. Campsites can be reserved in advance at Recreation.gov.

Just before completing the loop around the lake, the trail crosses a bridge over a flume. In 1916 the Hortonia Power Company, the predecessor to Central Vermont Public Service, built this concrete channel in order to divert water from Sucker Brook and Dutton Brook into Silver Lake and thus increase the volume of water flowing through its generators.

Complete the loop around the lake at 3.8 miles by passing through the picnic area and by the campground host. Retrace your steps down the service road, returning to the parking lot at 5.1 miles.

Miles and Directions

0.0 Start at the trailhead for Silver Lake and Rattlesnake Cliffs/Mount Moosalamoo.

0.5 WATERFALL! Above the Falls of Lana, the route to Rattlesnake Cliffs/Mount Moosalamoo departs to the left. Bear right (east), continuing up the dirt road toward Silver Lake.

1.3 LAKE! The road ends at the northern tip of Silver Lake at the Rocky Point Interpretive Trail. Bear right (west) to circumnavigate the lake.

1.9 The Chandler Ridge Trail enters from the right. Continue straight (south) on the interpretive trail next to the lake.

2.1 Pass over a small cave in the rocks.

2.8 Pass the junction with the Leicester Hollow Trail, which departs to the right.

3.1 Pass through the designated camping area on the east side of the lake.

3.8 Close the loop around the lake and retrace your steps down the dirt road.

5.1 Arrive back at the trailhead parking lot.

18 Rattlesnake Cliffs and Mount Moosalamoo

A serene woodland walk to a spectacular 160-foot waterfall, one of the tallest in Vermont, and the summit of a prominent peak in the region.

General location: Goshen
Distance: 6.2-mile lollipop
Hiking time: About 5.5 hours
Highest point: 2,640 feet
Elevation gain: 2,210 feet
Difficulty: Very strenuous (due to elevation gain)
When to go: Year-round, except during mud season
Canine compatibility: Dog friendly
Trail surface: Packed dirt, rocks, slab

Land status: Public
Trail users: Hikers, snowshoers
Water availability: Limited beyond the first mile
Map: USGS East Middlebury quad
Special considerations: The cliff area may be closed if peregrine falcons are nesting there.
Trail contact: Moosalamoo Association, (802) 989-6980, www.moosalamoo.org; Green Mountain National Forest, Rochester District, (802) 767-4261, www.fs.usda.gov/gmfl

Finding the trailhead: On the east side of Lake Dunmore, follow Route 53 for 0.2 mile south of Branbury State Park. Park at the trailhead. If full, there are three or four spots in front of boulder barricades along Route 53 between the parking lot and the state park.

The Hike

Moosalamoo is an Abenaki term that loosely translated means "he trails the moose" or "the moose departs." It was the original name of Lake Dunmore, then the mountain, and now the entire 22,000-acre region, which is bounded by Route 125 to the north through Middlebury Gap, Route 73 to the south, the Long Trail to the east down the main spine of the Green Mountains, and Route 53 to the west.

Mount Moosalamoo (pronounced *MOO-slah-moo)* is the highest peak in the area. It sees little foot traffic, is fairly smooth, and is not very steep above the cliffs, which makes for a pleasant hike through airy woods.

From the parking lot, walk up a short rise to a Forest Service access road, an unpaved lane that is not open to motorized traffic. Turn right, heading up the road, which soon passes under a huge pipe, called a penstock. Water from Silver Lake above travels through the penstock to a small hydroelectric power station on Route 53 below.

At 0.5 mile the road passes the top of the Falls of Lana. The falls are named for General John Ellis Wool, an officer in the US Army during the War of 1812, the Mexican-American War, and the American Civil War. General Wool came upon the Falls of Lana in 1850. *Lana* is the Spanish word for wool. Earlier, during his tour of duty in Mexico, General Wool became known as General Lana, a nickname that followed him to New England. The falls are fed by Sucker Brook, which is always

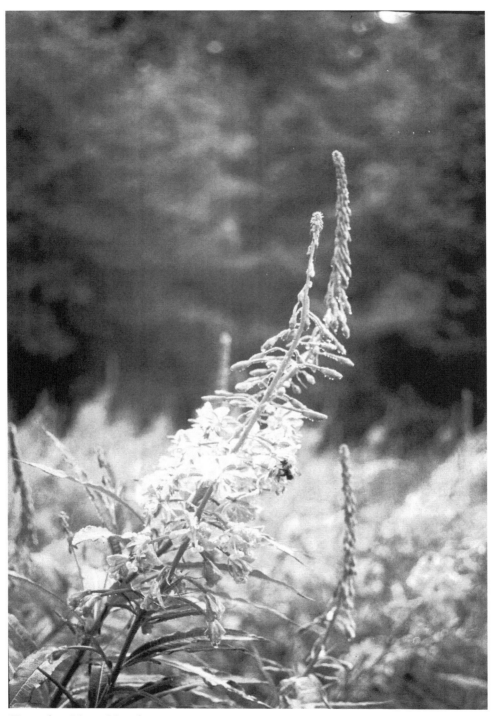

Fireweed on Mount Moosalamoo. Lisa Ballard

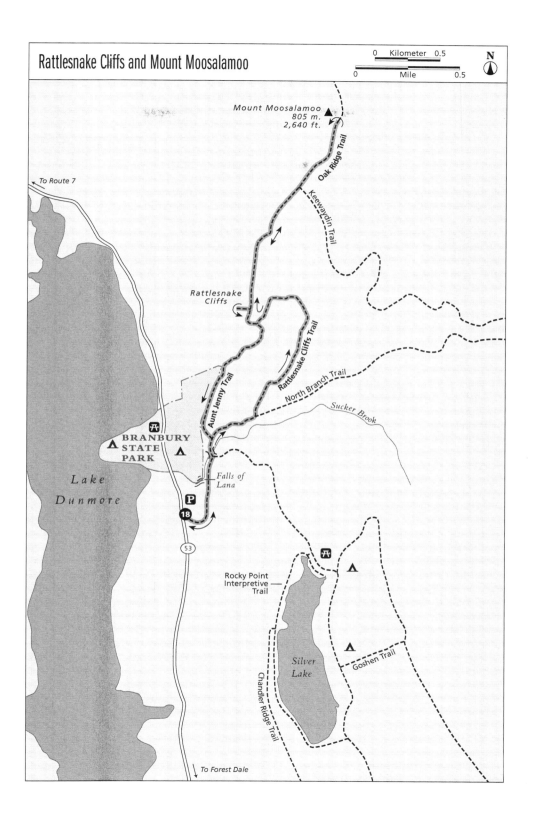

Rattlesnake Cliffs and Mount Moosalamoo

Mount Moosalamoo
805 m.
2,640 ft.

Oak Ridge Trail

Keewaydin Trail

Rattlesnake Cliffs

To Route 7

Rattlesnake Cliffs Trail

North Branch Trail

Sucker Brook

Aunt Jenny Trail

BRANBURY STATE PARK

Lake Dunmore

Falls of Lana

P

18

53

Rocky Point Interpretive Trail

Silver Lake

Goshen Trail

Chandler Ridge Trail

To Forest Dale

0   Kilometer   0.5

0   Mile   0.5

N

dramatic and often a raging torrent. Use care if you hike down toward the falls for a better look, as the roots are slick from constant spray.

From the top of the falls, the trail parallels Sucker Brook as it climbs gently to an intersection with the trail to Silver Lake. Go straight toward Rattlesnake Cliffs, aka Rattlesnake Point, continuing along the brook.

Soon the trail turns left again and crosses the brook via a well-constructed bridge. A primitive campsite is immediately on your right off the bridge, a nice choice if you prefer streamside camping to lake camping, which is available by Silver Lake.

Bear right at the intersection off the bridge onto the North Branch Trail. The trail is still wide here, but more like a footpath, as it leaves the stream.

At the next intersection, the Aunt Jenny Trail heads up to your left. This will be your return route. The trail is named for Jenny Rickert, who operated a tearoom near the power station in the early 1900s. Hikers often stopped there for refreshments en route to Rattlesnake Cliffs.

Continue straight for a short way, taking your next left on the Rattlesnake Cliffs Trail (blue blazes). The trail descends a ravine and crosses a stream at 1.4 miles, then ascends steeply through lush temperate forest. Eventually the trail narrows as it zigzags up the hillside, becoming less groomed. It also becomes less steep and soon crosses a stream that is often dry. It dips slightly and then traverses to the upper junction with the Aunt Jenny Trail at 2.1 miles.

From here the trail heads up again over rock steps, where you can catch glimpses of Lake Dunmore far below. A number of unofficial spurs lead to lookouts on the cliffs; however, if peregrine falcons are nesting (potentially from mid-March through early August), the cliff area will be closed. For that reason, it is best to contact the Forest Service before doing this hike if you want to be certain about visiting the cliff area.

In case you're an ophidiophobe (one who fears snakes), you will be relieved to learn that you are unlikely to encounter a rattler on Rattlesnake Cliffs. Although eastern timber rattlesnakes were common across Vermont centuries ago (and were likely the reason the cliffs are so named), today they are found in just a couple secluded preserves in western Rutland County.

At 2.4 miles the trail reaches an intersection with the official trail to the cliff top, called Rattlesnake Point. Turn left to reach the point, which, if open, offers a spectacular view of the lake below and the mountains beyond. Rattlesnake Cliffs is a popular destination, much more popular than the summit of Mount Moosalamoo. Most hikers do not go beyond this point, but it's worth continuing. The stretch to the summit is also quite rewarding. To reach the summit, return to the intersection with the main trail after visiting the cliffs and continue uphill.

The trail gradually gains altitude as it continues along a spine of rock separated from the cliffs by a thin band of forest. It is tempting to stare at the lake far below through the trees but keep an eye on the blue blazes and the trail. Grass obscures the path in places, which often seems more like a game trail than a hiking route. It is a worthwhile adventure. This pristine forest is home to migratory songbirds and seventeen rare plant species.

As the trail climbs away from the lake, it winds through classic upland woods in a generally northern direction. Do not be surprised if you suddenly flush a grouse.

At 2.8 miles the Keewaydin Trail enters from the right (southeast). Continue straight ahead toward the summit. The trail is now called the Oak Ridge Trail (blue blazes).

After a dozen steep rock steps, the trail passes to the right of a clearing, a false summit that contains a small hut and a solar panel. The path heads around the right side of the clearing, then at 3.1 miles breaks out on a small ledge, which is the summit. It is peppered with blueberry bushes and often moose scat. The summit of Moosalamoo is definitely an example of how the journey can be more interesting than the goal, but the view is pretty enough, primarily of nearby Sugar Hill on the next ridge to the east.

Return by the same route to the top of the Aunt Jenny Trail. Take the Aunt Jenny Trail to the North Branch Trail, returning to the trailhead parking lot at 6.2 miles.

Miles and Directions

0.0 Start at the trailhead for Silver Lake and Rattlesnake Cliffs/Mount Moosalamoo.

0.5 WATERFALL! Above the Falls of Lana, the route to Silver Lake departs to the right. Continue straight, following the brook, then turn left across the brook over the bridge. Bear right at the intersection off a footbridge onto the North Branch Trail.

2.4 CLIFFS! Bear left on a trail that goes to the cliff area, then retrace back to the Rattlesnake Cliffs Trail to continue to the summit. *Note:* Some trail signs and maps refer to the cliff area as "Rattlesnake Point" and others as "Rattlesnake Cliffs." It is the same place.

2.8 The Keewaydin Trail enters from the right (southeast). Continue straight on the Oak Ridge Trail.

3.1 SUMMIT! Arrive at the summit of Mount Moosalamoo. Return by the same route to the top of the Aunt Jenny Trail.

4.3 Just below Rattlesnake Point, turn right, continuing to descend via the Aunt Jenny Trail.

5.7 Turn right onto the North Branch Trail.

6.2 Arrive back at the trailhead.

19 Abbey Pond

A steady climb to a pristine mountain pond and a nice picnic spot on open rock by the water. Along the way, see an unusual assortment of boulders throughout the woods and a brook with many cascades and small pools. Very colorful during fall foliage season!

General location: East Middlebury
Distance: 4.4 miles out and back
Hiking time: About 3.5 hours
Highest point: 1,700 feet
Elevation gain: 1,200 feet
Difficulty: Moderate
When to go: Year-round
Canine compatibility: Dog friendly
Trail surface: Packed dirt, gravel, loose stones

Land status: Public
Nearest amenities: Middlebury
Trail users: Hikers, snowshoers
Water availability: Pond and brook
Map: USGS South Mountain quad
Special considerations: None
Trail contact: Green Mountain National Forest, Rochester District, (802) 767-4261, www.fs .usda.gov/gmfl

Finding the trailhead: From East Middlebury, head north on Route 116 toward Bristol for 4.2 miles. Turn right at the brown sign for the Abbey Pond Trail. The road forks immediately. Bear right and continue straight for 0.4 mile on this dirt road, which ends at the trailhead parking lot.

The Hike

The Abbey Pond Trail (blue blazes) enters the woods on a gravel path. At first, it climbs gently, with dense hardwood forest to either side and open sky above. At about 0.1 mile a boulder on your left grabs your attention, as it appears sliced into sections. More large boulders dot the woods. After crossing an old stone wall, the path becomes somewhat steeper and the gravel gives way to larger loose stones.

At 0.2 mile the trail crosses a scenic brook on a solid footbridge. Cascades tumble down a small gorge on the right, then flow over smooth ledges to the left. From here the climb continues on a moderate incline on a woods road, paralleling the brook. It is a lovely setting. The trail passes by more cascades, and the surrounding woods are dotted with interesting boulders and rocky outcroppings. Large trees cling impossibly to the tops of rocks.

At 0.6 mile the trail crosses the brook again, this time without a bridge, making the crossing somewhat tricky except in dry conditions. The driest route across is toward a narrow gap between two boulders on the opposite shore.

The trail continues along the hillside and then arcs right, away from the brook, before resuming its steady climb. A few minutes later, it bends back to the left past vernal pools, and the grade eases.

The path makes a long traverse, eventually returning to the brook. At about 1.4 miles the trail crosses the brook by a large shallow pool. It narrows to a traditional footpath, first arcing to the left, then snaking through the woods over flat terrain.

Abbey Pond

After a long traverse to the south, the trail crosses a muddy section and arrives at Abbey Pond at 2.2 miles. There is no path around the pond, but a large rocky outcropping on the right lends itself to picnicking. The pond's shoreline is dotted with beaver dams. Robert Frost Mountain graces the far shore. Abbey Pond is particularly pleasant during fall foliage season, when the entire shoreline turns red and orange.

Return by the same route.

Miles and Directions

0.0 Start at the trailhead for the Abbey Pond Trail.

0.1 Pass a boulder "sliced" into sections.

0.2 Cross a brook on a footbridge.

0.6 Recross the brook without a footbridge.

1.4 Cross the brook again.

2.2 POND! Return by the same route.

4.4 Arrive back at the trailhead.

◀ *The shoreline of Abbey Pond.* LISA BALLARD

20 Mount Abraham via the Long Trail

A relatively short but steady climb to an alpine summit on one of Vermont's 4,000-footers and an impressive 360-degree view.

General location: Warren
Distance: 5.2 miles out and back
Hiking time: About 4.5 hours
Highest point: 4,006 feet
Elevation gain: 1,700 feet
Difficulty: More challenging
When to go: Year-round, except during mud season
Canine compatibility: Dog friendly, though there's some scrambling up rock slab on the upper portion of the hike. No reliable water. Dogs must be on leash above tree line.
Trail surface: Packed dirt, rocky slab requiring some scrambling
Land status: Public
Trail users: Hikers, snowshoers
Water availability: None
Map: USGS Lincoln quad
Special considerations: None
Trail contact: Green Mountain Club, (802) 244-7037, www.greenmountainclub.org

Finding the trailhead: From Route 100 in Warren, take Lincoln Gap Road west toward Lincoln. This is a narrow, steep road that is closed during the winter. The trailhead is at the top of the gap. Park on either side of the road.

The Hike

Mount Abraham is the lowest of the five 4,000-foot peaks in Vermont. Likewise, it is the fifth-highest point in the state. It is a popular hike and relatively short for the big reward at the top, a view into three different states: New York to the west, New Hampshire to the east, and a significant portion of the spine of Vermont's Green Mountains to the north and south.

From the trailhead at Lincoln Gap, take the Long Trail (LT)–North (white blazes). The trail is flat at first and then dips through a depression as it meanders through the woods on the approach to Mount Abraham. At 0.4 mile the trail starts to climb. It also becomes rockier and more rooted, but nothing extreme. Periodic stone steps aid your footing. The trailhead is relatively high (2,531 feet), already in the boreal zone, and the path winds up through a typical boreal forest, primarily spruce, balsam, and birch. There are glimpses to the west through the trees.

After crossing two streams, the trail reaches the intersection with the Battell Trail, another common route up Mount Abraham, at 1.7 miles. Turn right, continuing on the LT–North to Battell Shelter at 1.8 miles. Both the trail and the shelter are named for Joseph Battell, a conservationist and former owner of the Bread Loaf Inn, who cut a trail to Mount Ellen in 1901. Battell Shelter is a simple lean-to with a picnic table. It is a convenient place to spend the night if you want to hike the entire ridge from

The Monroe Skyline from Mount Abraham, with Mansfield's Chin in the distance. MARK AIKEN

Lincoln Gap to Appalachian Gap. The Green Mountain Club charges a small fee per person per night. Campfires are not allowed.

From Battell Shelter, turn left to continue to the summit of Mount Abraham. Soon the trees get noticeably shorter and the trail turns to slab. The ascent is steeper here, but you can catch views to the northwest between deep breaths.

Just below the summit, as the trail passes through gnarled low pines indicative of the krummholz zone at tree line, notice the large white quartzite rock on the left side of the path. It looks like a giant egg.

At 2.6 miles the trail reaches the summit, with its 360-degree panorama. The White Mountains dominate the eastern skyline. To the west, you can see Bristol Cliffs, Lake Champlain, and the Adirondacks in the distance. To the south, the view takes you down the spine of the Green Mountains to Killington. Mount Mansfield pokes out beyond the shoulder of Mount Ellen to the north.

The top of Mount Abraham is home to one of only three alpine zones in Vermont. The other two are on Camel's Hump and Mount Mansfield. While the alpine zone on Mount Abraham is the smallest of the three peaks, about the size of a large living room, it is home to an array of fragile alpine plants that survive despite an abbreviated two-month growing season (mid-June to mid-August). The grass on the summit is not common grass, but rare Bigelow's sedge. Be careful to step on the rocks and not the sedge.

Return by the same route.

Mount Abraham via the Long Trail

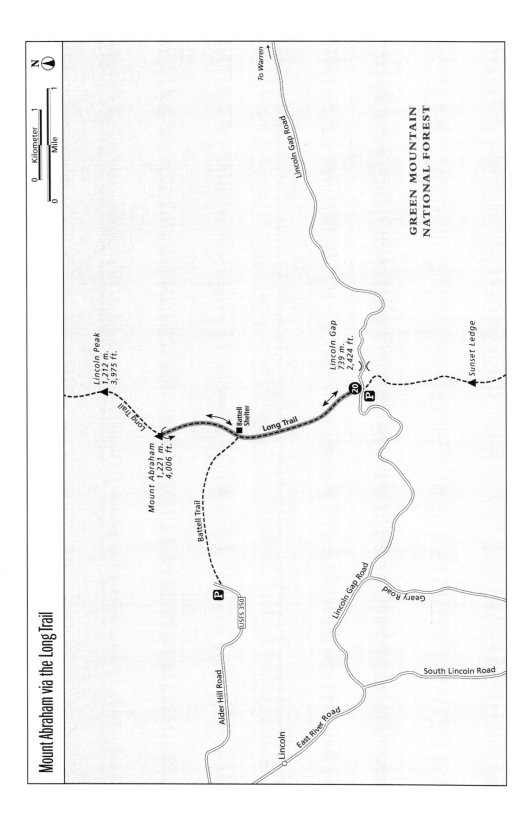

N

0   Kilometer   1

0   Mile   1

To Warren

Lincoln Gap Road

GREEN MOUNTAIN
NATIONAL FOREST

Lincoln Peak
1,212 m.
3,975 ft.

Long Trail

Mount Abraham
1,221 m.
4,006 ft.

Battell Shelter

Long Trail

Lincoln Gap
739 m.
2,424 ft.

20

Sunset Ledge

Battell Trail

USFS 350

Lincoln Gap Road

Geary Road

Alder Hill Road

South Lincoln Road

Lincoln

East River Road

LINCOLN GAP TO APPALACHIAN GAP

If you are looking for a longer hike and have two cars, it is worth hiking the entire ridge from Lincoln Gap to Appalachian Gap. This skywalk is a peak-bagger's delight, crossing at least four summits—Mount Abraham (elevation 4,006 feet), Lincoln Peak (3,972 feet), Mount Ellen (4,083 feet), and General Stark Mountain (3,662 feet). Some maps also recognize Nancy Hanks Peak on the north side of Lincoln Peak and Cutts Peak on the south side of Mount Ellen, which would give you six summits in one trip. Others consider the entire ridge to be only two peaks—Lincoln and Stark—with prominent points like Mount Abraham to be part of the other two. Regardless of how you count them, this hike is one of the classic ridge walks in Vermont.

The hike is on a section of the Long Trail, commonly called the Monroe Skyline in honor of Will Monroe, who played a key role in locating it here. The total vertical gain (2,520 feet) sounds high but feels reasonable because it is spread out over 11.6 miles. Half of the climb is at the start, to the top of Mount Abraham, which makes the remaining elevation gain hardly noticeable. From the summit of Mount Abraham, the route basically follows the ridgeline, rolling along to the north. That said, the mileage makes this trek formidable as a day hike for all but the fittest hikers.

If you are not up for an 11-mile day, or if you would like to combine the hike with a night in the woods, consider staying at Battell Shelter, 1.7 miles from the trailhead at Lincoln Gap, or at Dean Shelter, 1.8 miles above Appalachian Gap.

Leave one car on Route 17 at the top of Appalachian Gap, which is west of Route 100 in Waitsfield, then drive to the trailhead for Mount Abraham at the top of Lincoln Gap to begin the hike (see Hike 20, Mount Abraham via the Long Trail).

Another popular option: If you want slightly shorter mileage and a more-manageable car shuttle, the Monroe Skyline via Hikes 21 (Mount Abraham via the Battell Trail) and 22 (Mount Ellen via the Jerusalem Trail) is a 10.7-mile hike and just a twenty-minute drive from trailhead to trailhead.

Miles and Directions

0.0 Start at the trailhead for the LT–North.
0.4 Begin climbing.
1.7 Turn right at the junction with the Battell Trail, continuing on the LT–North.
1.8 Pass Battell Shelter.
2.5 Pass a large white quartzite "egg" near tree line.
2.6 SUMMIT! Return by the same route.
5.2 Arrive back at the trailhead.

21 Mount Abraham via the Battell Trail

A persistent ascent through four distinct climate zones to the summit of a 4,000-footer with an alpine summit that gives an expansive 360-degree view of the Adirondacks in New York, the White Mountains in New Hampshire, and a large portion of the Green Mountains in Vermont.

General location: Lincoln
Distance: 5.8 miles out and back
Hiking time: About 5.5 hours
Highest point: 4,006 feet
Elevation gain: 2,500 feet
Difficulty: Very strenuous (due to elevation gain)
When to go: Year-round, except during mud season
Canine compatibility: Dog friendly, though some scrambling up rock slab on the upper portion of hike. No reliable water. Dogs must be on leash in alpine zone above tree line.
Trail surface: Packed dirt, rocks, rocky slab in places
Land status: Public
Nearest amenities: Huntington
Trail users: Hikers, snowshoers, skiers
Water availability: None
Map: USGS Lincoln quad
Special considerations: None
Trail contact: Green Mountain Club, (802) 244-7037, www.greenmountainclub.org

Finding the trailhead: From the junction of River Road and Quaker Street in Lincoln, go 0.6 mile west on Quaker Street. Turn right (east) on Elder Hill Road and go 1.3 miles. Bear right on USFS Road 350 and go another mile. The trailhead and small parking area are on your left.

The Hike

The Battell Trail (blue blazes) is a popular route to the top of Mount Abraham, particularly if you are on the western side of Vermont. It is named for Joseph Battell, a conservationist, Morgan horse breeder, and former owner of the Bread Loaf Inn. Battell was born in 1839 in Middlebury, Vermont, and served both in the Vermont state legislature and as a trustee of Middlebury College. Unmarried, he bequeathed several large pieces of land to Middlebury College and to the State of Vermont and is thus credited with preserving substantial tracts of forest that hikers continue to enjoy today, including Camel's Hump State Park and the John Battell Wilderness south of the Breadloaf Wilderness. Middlebury College gradually transferred its portion of Battell's land to the USDA Forest Service between the 1930s and 1950s, which helped prompt the creation of the northern Green Mountain National Forest.

The Battell Trail is a slightly longer route to the summit of Mount Abraham than the Long Trail (LT) from Lincoln Gap, but it is interesting because it passes through four distinct climate zones, which the LT does not.

The Battell Trail begins as a smooth footpath through a hardwood forest, with ferns carpeting the sides of the path. At first, the route is a moderate stroll with some

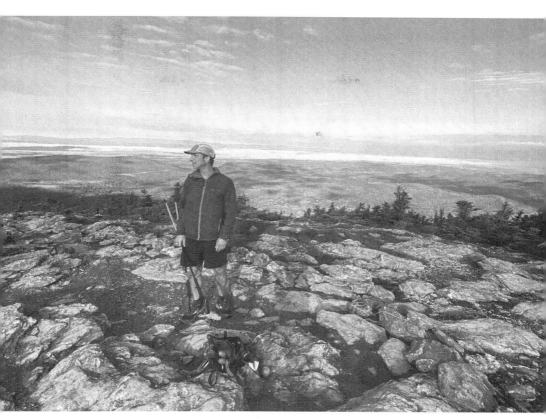

An autumn morning in the alpine zone on Mount Abraham. MARK AIKEN

short, steep inclines. The stroll is short-lived, however. By 0.2 mile the ascent becomes persistent, winding up the western flank of the mountain.

At 0.6 mile the footing becomes noticeably rougher and more rooted, though the angle of ascent eases on a traverse to the south. After crossing two brooks on raised puncheons, the trail becomes smooth again, angling upward to the southeast.

At 1.1 miles the trail bends sharply to the left (north). A few minutes later, it enters the boreal zone—predominantly softwoods. Moss and rocks dot the trail, which resembles a dry streamlet. After a short while, the trail reaches a plateau, and the footing improves. It continues uphill, but on a more moderate incline.

At 2.0 miles the Battell Trail ends at the LT. Continue on the LT–North (white blazes), passing Battell Shelter a little farther up the trail. Battell Shelter is a three-sided lean-to. There is a picnic table and a nearby tent platform for use if the shelter is full. Walk along the left side of the shelter to continue to the summit.

The climb remains gentle until it reaches a series of elongated steps. From here it is a steady uphill ascent. After crossing a length of slab, a view of the summit appears ahead. With each successive piece of slab, the views become bigger, with panoramas soon opening to the south and east. The boreal forest gives way to the krummholz

Mount Abraham via the Battell Trail

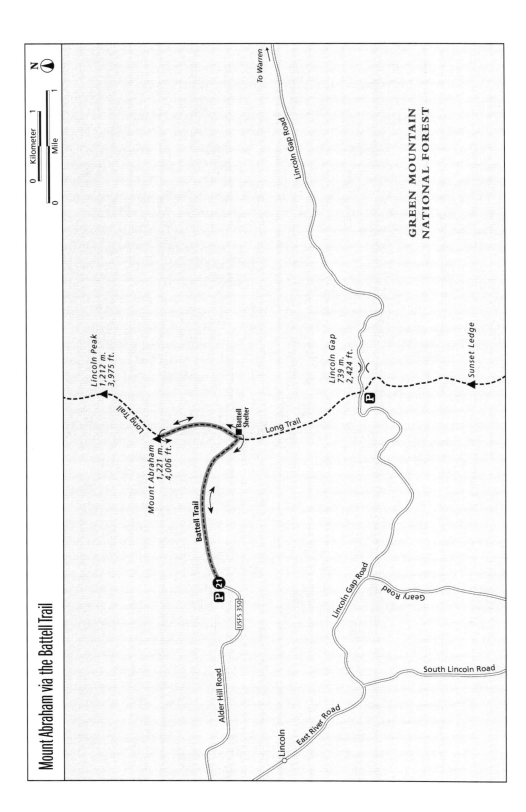

N

0 — Kilometer — 1
0 — Mile — 1

Lincoln Peak
1,212 m.
3,975 ft.

Long Trail

Mount Abraham
1,221 m.
4,006 ft.

Battell Shelter

Battell Trail

Long Trail

P 21

USFS 350

Alder Hill Road

Lincoln

East River Road

Lincoln Gap Road

Geary Road

South Lincoln Road

Lincoln Gap
739 m.
2,424 ft.

P

Lincoln Gap Road

To Warren

Sunset Ledge

GREEN MOUNTAIN
NATIONAL FOREST

zone, where stunted gnarled trees grow just at tree line. After scrambling up three short "chimneys" of rock, the trail passes a huge white quartzite "egg" and then arrives at the bare summit.

The summit of Mount Abraham is in the alpine zone, typical of the arctic tundra a thousand miles to the north. It is one of only three alpine zones in Vermont. The other two are on Camel's Hump and Mount Mansfield. While the alpine zone on Mount Abraham is the smallest of the three peaks, about the size of a large living room, it is home to an array of fragile alpine plants that survive despite an abbreviated two-month growing season (mid-June to mid-August). The grass on the summit is not common grass, but rare Bigelow's sedge. Be careful to step on the rocks and not the sedge.

Return by the same route.

Miles and Directions

0.0 Start at the trailhead for the Battell Trail.

0.6 Cross two brooks on puncheons.

1.1 Bend sharply left (north) and enter boreal forest.

2.0 The Battell Trail ends at the LT. Turn left onto the LT-North.

2.1 Pass Battell Shelter.

2.9 SUMMIT! Return by the same route.

5.8 Arrive back at the trailhead.

22 Mount Ellen via the Jerusalem Trail

A short, steep hike through an operating maple sugar bush to a unique ridge walk and eventually a 4,000-foot peak.

General location: Starksboro
Distance: 8.6 miles out and back
Hiking time: About 6.5 hours
Highest point: 4,083 feet
Elevation gain: 2,505 feet
Difficulty: Very strenuous (due to elevation gain and mileage)
When to go: Year-round, except during mud season
Canine compatibility: Dog friendly

Trail surface: Packed dirt, puncheons, rocks, mud
Land status: Private and public
Nearest amenities: Huntington
Trail users: Hikers, snowshoers
Water availability: Brook by trailhead
Map: USGS Mount Ellen quad
Special considerations: None
Trail contact: Green Mountain Club, (802) 244-7037, www.greenmountainclub.org

Finding the trailhead: From the intersection of Gore Road and Route 17 in Starksboro, go south on Route 17 for 3.7 miles. Turn left (east) on Jerusalem Road. Go 1.2 miles, then turn left (north) on Jim Dwire Road. The trailhead is a pullout on the right side of the road 0.5 mile after the turn onto Jim Dwire Road.

The Hike

Mount Ellen is tied with Camel's Hump as the third-highest peak in Vermont, although Ellen—with no alpine zone, a wooded summit, and a less recognizable profile—makes less of a splash than its equally elevated and more famous twin. Still, this hike to the highest point on the ridge known as the Monroe Skyline is quite challenging and rewarding in its own right, with views of Lake Champlain, the Adirondacks, and the Mad River Valley.

The Jerusalem Trail (blue blazes) starts on the right (east) side of Jim Dwire Road and immediately crosses a brook—the only water source on the entire route. The trail traverses through conifers and then a scrubby, overgrown hardwood forest before crossing a work road at 0.8 mile. Duck under a superhighway of sap lines as you enter a working maple sugar bush. The trail becomes a double-track here, wide enough for sugaring vehicles and equipment. The large, well-spaced maples, connected by sap lines, have little undergrowth with which to compete.

The Green Mountain Club (GMC) manages the Jerusalem Trail, much of which falls on private land that is actively logged and sugared. There is no camping allowed on this trail. The GMC stresses the importance of staying on the trail and respecting the private landowner. The differences in forest health where the forest is managed (above the sap lines) and not (below) are obvious as you climb.

Jogging along the Monroe Skyline north of Mount Ellen en route to the Jerusalem Trail.
MARK AIKEN

Mount Ellen via the Jerusalem Trail

Kilometers
0   2

Miles
0   2

N

To Starksboro

17

Long Trail

Jerusalem Trail

Orvis Lookout

22

Jim Dwire Road

Jerusalem Road

Jerusalem Road

Long Trail

Mount Ellen

Cutts Peak

Downingsville Road

Nancy Hanks Peak

Lincoln Peak

Mount Abraham

Battell Trail

Battell Shelter

Lincoln Gap Road

To Lincoln

17

The trail narrows again at 1.3 miles and enters a birch glade. It ascends steadily before coming to a flat spot, at 2.1 miles, in a stand of giant, gnarled birches. Here the trail steepens as the vegetation gives way to the stunted, twisted krummholz.

At 2.3 miles the Jerusalem Trail ends at a junction with the Long Trail (LT). Twenty steps to the left of the junction is Orvis Lookout, a rocky outcrop that looks west over Lake Champlain, affording views of Whiteface Mountain and Mount Marcy, two iconic peaks in the Adirondacks. Our route, however, goes right on the LT–South (white blazes) along a portion of the Monroe Skyline, the nickname for the classic 15-mile ridge from Lincoln Gap to Appalachian Gap.

Bright moss surrounds the trail here, and the trail surface alternates between rock and mud. In the muddiest sections, hikers have tossed sticks and dead wood in unofficial attempts to create puncheons. The trail continues gently upward until a rocky scramble at 3.6 miles, after which you enter the Green Mountain National Forest.

At 4.2 miles the trail breaks out of the gnarled, dense krummholz into a clearing at the top of Sugarbush Resort's Summit Quad chairlift, where you'll find the best views of the hike, including General Stark Mountain to the north with Mount Mansfield and Camel's Hump in the distance beyond, the Adirondacks to the west, and on clear days, New Hampshire to the east and Canada to the far north. Avoid venturing near the chairlift's unloading platform. The lift may turn even during the summertime. The viewless Mount Ellen summit is a short distance beyond the chairlift clearing.

Return by the same route.

Miles and Directions

0.0 Start at the trailhead for the Jerusalem Trail.

0.8 Cross a work road and duck beneath sap lines as the trail enters a maple sugar bush.

1.3 The trail narrows and ascends gently.

2.1 The trail steepens at a stand of giant birches.

2.3 ORVIS LOOKOUT! After taking in the view, turn right onto the LT-South.

4.2 VIEW! The trail breaks out into a clearing at Sugarbush ski area's Summit Quad chairlift.

4.3 SUMMIT! Return by the same route.

8.6 Arrive back at the trailhead.

23 Mount Philo

A popular local favorite and an easy up-and-back, with a huge, rewarding view of Lake Champlain and the Adirondacks.

General location: Charlotte
Distance: 1.6 miles out and back
Hiking time: About 1.5 hours
Highest point: 968 feet
Elevation gain: 580 feet
Difficulty: Easy
When to go: Year-round
Canine compatibility: Dog friendly. Dogs must be leashed at the summit picnic area, and bear in mind, it's a heavily trafficked trail.
Trail surface: Packed dirt, wooden steps, some rocks

Land status: Public
Trail users: Hikers, snowshoers
Water availability: Running water at summit parking lot
Map: USGS Mount Philo quad
Special considerations: A small fee is collected at the state park entrance.
Trail contact: Mount Philo State Park, (802) 425-2390, www.vtstateparks.com/philo.html; Vermont Department of Forests, Parks and Recreation, (802) 786-0060, www.fpr.vermont.gov

Finding the trailhead: From the junction of US 7 and State Park Road in Charlotte, follow State Park Road west for a mile to Mount Philo Road. Cross Mount Philo Road and pay the nominal fee at the park entrance. Parking is on the left. The trailhead is behind the gatehouse.

The Hike

Mount Philo is an understandably popular destination among Burlington-area locals. Few hikes offer such a beautiful panorama for such little effort.

Mount Philo State Park was Vermont's first state park. In 1924, Frances Humphreys gifted the property to the state. During the late 1800s, Frances and her husband, James, a wealthy couple from Massachusetts, stayed at an inn near the base of the mountain. They fell in love with the location and began purchasing property there, including the mountain, where they summered for a number of years. At the time, a carriage road led to the summit, where a springhouse, a gazebo, and other structures were built. The remains of these original buildings and the carriage road still exist.

The mountaintop is highly developed, so don't expect solitude. The current auto road, parking area, pavilion, picnic area, and ranger cabin were built during the 1930s by the Depression-era Civilian Conservation Corps and are still in use today. What you can expect is a nice hike through a hardwood forest, a grassy picnic area, and million-dollar views.

The House Rock Trail (blue blazes) leaves the trailhead behind the park entrance structure. It switchbacks before winding between two house-sized boulders at 0.2 mile. More likely than not, there will be young hikers climbing on the boulders

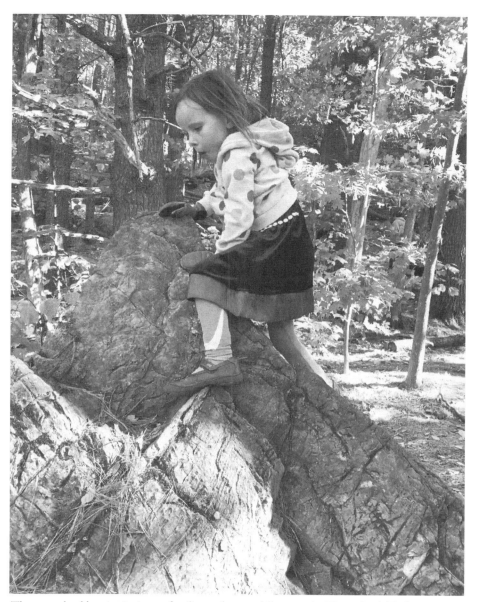

The many boulders, intriguing to families and young hikers, on the House Rock Trail.
MARK AIKEN

while their parents wait. These giant rocks have such nice steps and holds, you may be tempted to climb too.

The trail heads left and ascends some log steps before bending around a large rocky overhang. At 0.4 mile you climb more wooden steps and then another steep switchback.

At the top of the switchback, you step onto the auto road. Walk left (north) a few steps to get back on the trail. Ignore the spur to the right: It's another trail called the Devil's Chair Trail, an alternative (and less traveled) route to the summit that requires some walking along the paved road. Our route continues straight before turning sharply uphill at 0.6 mile. Ascend over well-maintained switchbacks, ignoring a spur to the left that leads to the campground. Arrive at the summit at 0.8 mile.

From the summit perch, Lake Champlain lies before you in full glory. The Adirondacks stand across the lake, with Bald Peak and Split Rock Mountain rising directly from Champlain's western shoreline. The Adirondack High Peaks loom in the distance, including Giant, Hurricane, and Whiteface Mountains. On this side of the lake, the Green Mountains stretch to the south, including Snake Mountain, Buck Mountain, and, farther away to the east, Mount Abraham, Mount Ellen, and the Monroe Skyline.

There are plenty of views from the grassy picnic area too, where you'll undoubtedly share the space with other hikers of all ages. Enjoy the views and the people-watching, then descend by the same route.

Miles and Directions

0.0 Start at the trailhead for the House Rock Trail.

0.2 Pass two large boulders.

0.5 Cross the auto road. Walk left for a few steps to get back on the trail, ignoring the Devil's Chair Trail.

0.6 Turn sharply uphill, then ascend switchbacks.

0.8 SUMMIT! Descend by the same route.

1.6 Arrive back at the trailhead.

Lake Champlain and the Adirondacks from Mount Philo summit. MARK AIKEN

Waterbury-Stowe Area

Waterbury to Jeffersonville

24 Camel's Hump via the Monroe Trail

Eastern approach to the summit of a landmark 4,000-footer, where you'll find a 360-degree view from the open rock summit and rare alpine flora.

General location: Duxbury
Distance: 6.8 miles out and back
Hiking time: About 5.5 hours
Highest point: 4,083 feet
Elevation gain: 1,800 feet
Difficulty: More challenging
When to go: Year-round, except during mud season
Canine compatibility: Dog friendly. Dogs should be on leash and on the trail (rocks) in alpine zone.

Trail surface: Packed dirt, rocks, some scrambling over rocks and slab
Land status: Public
Nearest amenities: Waterbury
Trail users: Hikers, snowshoers, skiers
Water availability: None
Map: USGS Huntington quad
Special considerations: None
Trail contact: Vermont Department of Forests, Parks and Recreation, (802) 879-6565, www .fpr.vermont.gov; Green Mountain Club, (802) 244-7037, www.greenmountainclub.org

Finding the trailhead: From Route 100/Main Street in Waterbury, turn southwest on Winooski Street. Cross over the Winooski River, then turn right (northwest) on River Road toward North Duxbury. Go 4.3 miles, then turn left (south) on Camel's Hump Road (no sign), which turns to dirt. At the fork, bear right over a bridge following the Hump sign. At the junction of View Trail and Summit Trail, bear right, following the sign for Summit Trail, which ends at the trailhead parking area.

The Hike

Camel's Hump is a Vermont icon. Its bald summit comes to an offset point, which is visible for miles on a clear day. The mountain has had many names over the centuries. The precolonial Native Americans called it *Tawabodi-e-wadso,* or "the saddle mountain." In the early 1600s, when Samuel de Champlain first saw the mountain while exploring the region for Henry IV of France, he thought it looked like a sleeping lion and thus dubbed it *Le Lion Couchant,* or "the couching lion." In the late 1700s, Ira Allen, Ethan Allen's brother, dubbed it Camel's Rump, which was later changed to a more gentlemanly Camel's Hump.

Though one of the highlights of the Long Trail (LT) for through-hikers, the two main approaches to Camel's Hump as a day hike are not on the LT, but from the southwest via the Burrows and Forest City Trails, and from the east via the Monroe Trail. The Monroe Trail (blue blazes), described here, is slightly longer and ascends at a moderate rate, with good footing most of the way. *Note:* Camel's Hump is a popular climb, so save this one for midweek if you can.

Enter the woods at the end of the parking area. The trail is smooth, with intermittent log water bars. It climbs gently at first through a mixed northern forest for about

Camel's Hump via the Monroe Trail

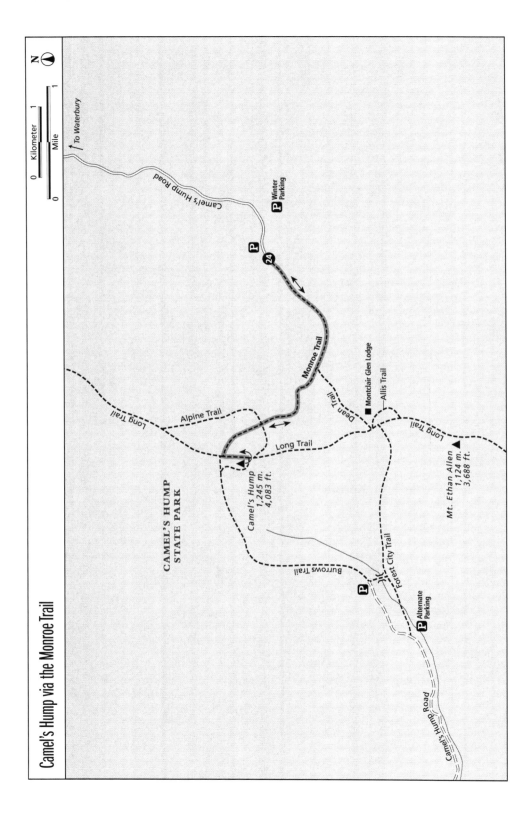

CAMEL'S HUMP
STATE PARK

Camel's Hump
1,245 m.
4,083 ft.

Mt. Ethan Allen
1,124 m.
3,688 ft.

Long Trail

Alpine Trail

Long Trail

Monroe Trail

Dean Trail

Allis Trail

Long Trail

Burrows Trail

Forest City Trail

Montclair Glen Lodge

Camel's Hump Road

Camel's Hump Road

To Waterbury

Winter Parking

Alternate Parking

24

N

0   Kilometer   1
0   Mile   1

View from the summit of Camel's Hump, looking south along the Monroe Skyline. LISA BALLARD

0.3 mile, then ascends more purposefully, crossing several well-constructed bridges along the way. The footing remains good, though more rocky as you gain altitude.

At 1.3 miles the trail comes to the junction with the Dean Trail. Bear right (northwest), staying on the Monroe Trail. The ascent eases for a bit, then continues upward more persistently again.

At 2.0 miles the trail crosses some rock slab, then becomes flatter and smoother until it enters softwoods. At this point, the path winds upward and becomes rocky again.

At 2.5 miles the Monroe Trail crosses the Alpine Trail. Continue straight ahead (north) on the Monroe Trail.

At 3.1 miles the trail comes to a clearing and another four-way junction with the Burrows Trail and the LT. The Monroe Trail ends at this junction. Turn left, following the LT–South into the alpine zone. From here it is an easy rock scramble for the last quarter mile. As you clear the tree line, look behind for views of Mount Mansfield.

The trail reaches the summit at 3.4 miles. The 360-degree view is nothing short of phenomenal. On a clear day, you can see west across the Champlain Valley to the Adirondacks, east to the White Mountains, and north and south along the high spine of the Green Mountains.

Return by the same route.

Miles and Directions

0.0 Start at the trailhead for the Monroe Trail.

1.3 Bear right (northwest) at the junction with the Dean Trail, continuing on the Monroe Trail.

2.5 Cross the Alpine Trail, continuing on the Monroe Trail.

3.1 Turn left onto the LT-South, entering the alpine zone.

3.4 SUMMIT! Return by the same route.

6.8 Arrive back at the trailhead.

25 Camel's Hump via the Forest City Trail– Burrows Trail Loop

Loop hike over a landmark 4,000-footer, with three ledges to climb on the way up and a 360-degree panorama from the rock summit.

General location: Huntington Center
Distance: 5.7-mile loop
Hiking time: About 5 hours
Highest point: 4,083 feet
Elevation gain: 1,950 feet
Difficulty: More challenging
When to go: Year-round, except during mud season
Canine compatibility: Some dogs will be challenged by the ledges on the way up. Be prepared to show proof of rabies vaccine to enter Camel's Hump State Park if a ranger is on duty. Dogs must be on leash in the state park at the trailhead, around the Montclair Glen Lodge, and in the alpine zone around the summit.

Trail surface: Packed dirt, rocks, slab, ledges requiring some scrambling
Land status: Public
Nearest amenities: Huntington
Trail users: Hikers, snowshoers, skiers
Water availability: Brush Brook on lower portion of route, then a stream near Montclair Glen Lodge
Map: USGS Huntington quad
Special considerations: None
Trail contact: Camel's Hump State Park, www .vtstateparks.com/camelshump.html; Vermont Department of Forests, Parks and Recreation, (802) 879-6565, www.fpr.vermont.gov; Green Mountain Club, (802) 244-7037, www.green mountainclub.org

Finding the trailhead: In Huntington Center, turn onto Camel's Hump Road and follow the signs for about 3.6 miles. Go past the first trailhead for the Forest City Trail. The best starting point and parking are at the upper parking lot.

The Hike

Camel's Hump is sizable in looks and in effort, but well worth the challenge. The mountain can be approached via the Long Trail (LT), but day hikers prefer to climb from either Duxbury on the eastern flank of the mountain or from Huntington on the western side. The Huntington side, described here, is about a mile shorter but arguably more challenging because of the "Stairs," a series of three consecutive ledges that require some minor scrambling. Most hikers will delight in the Stairs, which give you early views and add some topographical interest to the climb. The route described here also makes a loop, ascending via the Forest City Trail, where the Stairs are located (easier to climb up than down), and descending via the Burrows Trail. The Forest City Trail is a half mile longer than the Burrows Trail and offers numerous views of the summit during the last third of the climb.

From the trailhead, take the short connector over a bridge to the Forest City Trail (blue blazes). At the intersection with the Forest City Trail, turn left (northeast). The

Montclair Glen Lodge on Camel's Hump. LISA BALLARD

sizable stream, which eventually becomes Brush Brook, will remain on your right for a while as you climb steadily through the northern hardwood forest.

Because of its distinct ecological zones that continue all the way to the summit, Camel's Hump is the site of ongoing environmental studies and research. In 1965 the National Park Service named the mountain a National Natural Landmark. Research on Camel's Hump played an instrumental role in linking the effects of pollutants from the Midwest to deforestation in New England, which ultimately contributed to the creation of the Clean Air Act.

At 1.5 miles the Forest City Trail ends at a fork with the Long Trail (white blazes) to the left and the short spur to the Montclair Glen Lodge to the right. Built in 1948, the lodge is a small, cabin-like shelter typical of the LT, with plywood sleeping "shelves" and a table. The short trail to the cabin crosses a reliable brook. Space is available on a first-come, first-served basis. A Green Mountain Club backcountry caretaker, in residence from May through November, collects the per-person overnight fee.

To continue to the summit, stay on the LT–North. At 1.6 miles the trail comes to a three-way intersection with the Dean Trail and the Allis Trail. Turn left, continuing on the LT–North. The trail now becomes noticeably steeper and rockier as you get a glimpse of the neighboring Allen Range to the right (south).

From here the trail ascends the first "stair," affording the first real view. The trail passes two enormous boulders that rest against each other to form a tunnel. Take the tunnel or walk around it to the left. From the third stair, you can see the Hump, which seems surprisingly far away.

After the Stairs, the trail dips into a saddle as it approaches the summit cone. You will have frequent views of the Hump, like an imposing wall looming ahead through breaks in the low evergreen canopy.

Camel's Hump via the Forest City Trail–Burrows Trail Loop

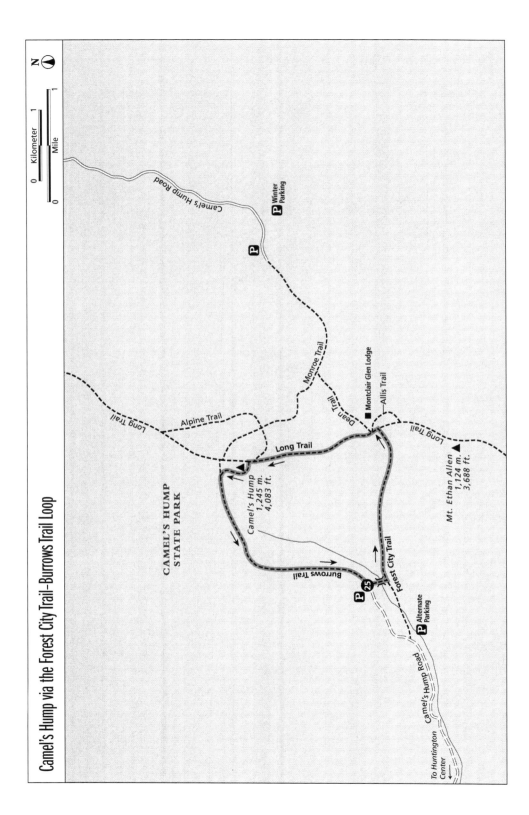

N

0   Kilometer   1

0   Mile   1

Camel's Hump Road

To Huntington Center

Alternate Parking

P 25

Forest City Trail

Burrows Trail

Camel's Hump
1,245 m.
4,083 ft.

CAMEL'S HUMP
STATE PARK

Long Trail

Alpine Trail

Long Trail

Monroe Trail

Dean Trail

Montclair Glen Lodge

Allis Trail

Long Trail

Mt. Ethan Allen
1,124 m.
3,688 ft.

Camel's Hump Road

Winter Parking

P

At 2.8 miles the LT meets the Alpine Trail, a connector to the Monroe Trail from the Duxbury side of the mountain and the summit bypass in case of bad weather. From this point, you are in the fragile alpine zone.

At 3.0 miles the LT reaches the summit of Camel's Hump. The low flora amid the rocks is similar to rare plant life found near the Arctic Circle. A number of the slow-growing plants here are on the endangered species list and are extremely sensitive to trampling. Much of the year, a caretaker is stationed on the summit to educate hikers about the fragile vegetation. Once on the summit, please stay on the rocks while you enjoy the endless 360-degree view.

To descend via the Burrows Trail, continue on the LT–North (do not retrace your steps). At 3.3 miles you will reach a clearing and another three-way intersection. This is the site of a former guesthouse that was a popular destination during the Civil War. However, its popularity waned with the development of Mount Mansfield and the Stowe area. At the clearing, turn left (west) onto the Burrows Trail (blue blazes).

Descend via the Burrows Trail, closing the loop at the trailhead at 5.7 miles.

Miles and Directions

0.0 Start on the connector trail, over a bridge, to the Forest City Trail.

1.5 The Forest City Trail ends at the LT. Turn left on the LT–North.

1.6 At the three-way intersection with the Dean Trail and the Allis Trail, turn left, continuing on the LT–North, climbing the three "stairs" (ledges).

2.8 Enter the alpine zone on the LT–North, continuing across the broad expanse of exposed rock.

3.0 SUMMIT! Descend by continuing on the LT–North.

3.3 Turn left (west) onto the Burrows Trail at the three-way intersection in a small clearing.

5.7 Close loop at the trailhead.

26 Stimson Mountain via the Long Trail

A beautiful forest hike on the newest section of Vermont's oldest trail.

General location: Bolton
Distance: 10.2 miles out and back
Hiking time: About 6.5 hours
Highest point: 2,308 feet
Elevation gain: 1,800 feet
Difficulty: Very strenuous (due to mileage). This hike can be made shorter by turning back at a lookout at mile 3.7.
When to go: Year-round, except during mud season
Canine compatibility: Dog friendly. Dogs should be on a leash as you pass through the Lower West Bolton rock-climbing crag.

Trail surface: Packed dirt, a few areas of slabby rock
Land status: Public
Nearest amenities: Richmond or Waterbury
Trail users: Hikers, snowshoers
Water availability: None
Map: USGS Richmond quad
Special considerations: None
Trail contact: Green Mountain Club, (802) 244-7037, www.greenmountainclub.org

Finding the trailhead: From the junction of US 2 and Brown's Trace Road in Richmond, follow US 2 east for 4.8 miles to the Long Trail parking area on the left (north) side of the road. From the rotary at the junction of Route 100 and US 2 in Waterbury, follow US 2 west 8.4 miles to the Long Trail parking area on the right (north) side of the road.

The Hike

If you've ever wondered what sort of trail $2.3 million buys, hike the Long Trail to Stimson Mountain. That is the amount the Green Mountain Club (GMC) raised for a comprehensive trail rerouting and construction project that secured a reliable route across the Winooski River for through-hikers coming off Camel's Hump. Prior to this new stretch of the Long Trail (LT), hikers had to walk 3 miles along a road to get to the nearest river crossing. Most of the money funded the construction of a 224-foot steel suspension bridge over the river. The project was the largest, most ambitious, most expensive, most complicated, and most protracted in GMC history. To illustrate how long this issue was on the club's radar, the Vermont state legislature appropriated $500 in 1916 to resolve the problem of the Winooski River crossing, a laughable amount considering the project's final price tag, even considering a century of inflation.

This route doesn't put you on the summit of Stimson Mountain, although there are tentative GMC plans for an eventual side trail to the top. However, it takes you through a diverse forest and across a unique ridgeline with views of Lake Champlain, the Adirondacks, and the Bolton Valley ski area. And it's a celebration of the doggedness and commitment of the Green Mountain Club, American's oldest trail stewardship organization, to complete a project that included conserving 300 acres of land, engineering a bridge, crossing a railroad, accessing a tunnel beneath an interstate, navigating an intersection at a popular rock-climbing area, and cutting 5 new miles of footpath. The project was completed in 2015, and the trail reroute is the hike described here.

From the trailhead, the Long Trail (white blazes) parallels US 2 on a gravel track for 0.3 mile. Turn right on Notch Road and go through the tunnel under the interstate, the only time in this guidebook where you're advised to watch for cars. At 0.6 mile turn right on the LT and descend a thirteen-step wooden ladder/stairway.

The trail comes to Lower West Bolton crag at 0.8 mile. Unless you are hiking in the dead of winter, you are likely to encounter rock climbers on this 130-foot cliff. If you are hiking with a dog, keeping your canine pal under control here is a matter of life or death for the climbers on belay! The trail parallels the base of the cliff band and then turns steeply uphill to an intersection with the Climbers Path, on the left, at the top of the cliffs. Take the right fork, staying on the LT, which enters the Mount Mansfield State Forest at 1.0 mile.

The trail ascends gently but steadily through well-spaced hardwoods. At 1.4 miles the LT joins a former logging road and then crosses a stream. The hike's biggest vertical gain begins here, but the longest set of switchbacks on the entire Long Trail eases the pain.

From the top of the switchbacks, at 1.9 miles, you descend slightly and then cross a fern-filled clearing where you can look up the shoulder of Stimson Mountain, which looms another 400 feet above. Be careful to stay on the trail here, as the ferns are intermingled with nettles.

From here the trail rolls over slight ups and downs as it traverses a hardwood forest along Stimson Ridge, crossing a logging road at 2.8 miles. Although viewpoints are sparse, the walking is smooth and pleasant, and the mixed hardwoods are beautiful, especially during the fall foliage season. A spur trail on the left (northwest) at 3.7 miles brings you to an unnamed lookout across Bolton Notch, the Winooski River Valley, Lake Champlain, and New York State's Adirondacks. It's a perfect spot for a snack or, for some, a turnaround, as this lookout is a worthy destination in its own right.

At 4.1 miles the trail turns sharply to the southeast as you ascend another set of switchbacks onto Oxbow Ridge. Heading north along the ridge, you can glimpse Bolton Valley ski area and its white village nestled at the feet of Bolton Mountain and Ricker Peak to the east.

At 5.1 miles you come to a trail junction with the "Old Long Trail," also called Duck Brook Trail. This is the route through-hikers on the LT used to take before the bridge over the Winooski River was built.

This is the end of the newest (and most expensive) section of the LT. You can turn this hike into a loop if you follow the Duck Brook Trail 5.4 miles back to US 2. Keep in mind, you would then need to walk 1.3 miles along US 2 to complete the loop, a long day to be sure. Or return the way you came. To see the new suspension

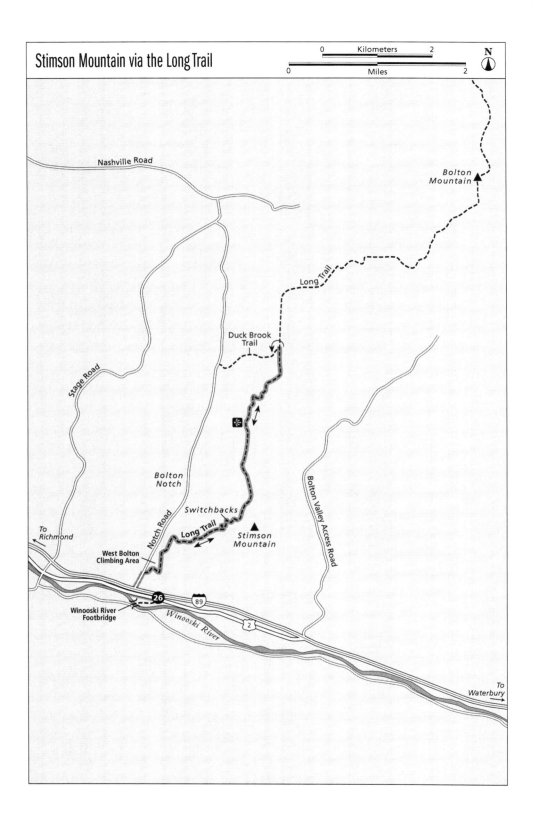

Stimson Mountain via the Long Trail

Nashville Road

Bolton
Mountain

Long Trail

Duck Brook
Trail

Stage Road

Bolton Valley Access Road

Bolton
Notch

Switchbacks

Notch Road

Long Trail

Stimson
Mountain

To
Richmond

West Bolton
Climbing Area

26 89

Winooski River
Footbridge

Winooski River

2

To
Waterbury

0   Kilometers   2
0   Miles   2

N

bridge, which is not part of this hike, cross US 2 at the parking area and walk a short 0.2 mile to the bridge.

Miles and Directions

0.0 Start at the trailhead for the Long Trail. The trail initially parallels US 2.

0.3 Turn right onto Notch Road, going through a tunnel under the interstate.

0.6 Turn right onto the LT.

0.8 Pass by Lower West Bolton crag.

1.0 At the top of the rock-climbing cliff, take the right fork away from cliff.

1.4 Climb up switchbacks.

1.9 Take in the view up the shoulder of Stimson Mountain. Continue on the LT.

3.7 LOOKOUT! Bear left onto a spur trail to an impressive viewpoint.

5.1 Junction with the "Old Long Trail." Return by the same route.

10.2 Arrive back at the trailhead.

27 Mount Hunger via the Waterbury Trail

A short, steep hike that's a favorite among locals and that ends at a spectacular bald mountaintop.

General location: Waterbury Center
Distance: 4.4 miles out and back (with optional 1.2-mile out-and-back to White Rock Mountain)
Hiking time: About 4.5 hours (add 0.5 hour for hike to White Rock Mountain)
Highest point: 3,538 feet
Elevation gain: 2,290 feet
Difficulty: Very strenuous (due to elevation gain)
When to go: Year-round, except during mud season
Canine compatibility: For agile dogs only. Inexperienced dogs, small dogs, and senior dogs will be challenged on the ledgy sections on the upper mountain.
Trail surface: Variable, packed dirt, rocks, ledgy sections requiring easy scrambling
Land status: Public
Nearest amenities: Waterbury
Trail users: Hikers, snowshoers
Water availability: Seasonal streams, reliable cascade about a mile into hike
Map: USGS Stowe quad
Special considerations: None
Trail contact: Vermont Department of Forests, Parks and Recreation, (802) 476-0182, www.fpr.vermont.gov; Green Mountain Club, (802) 244-7037, www.greenmountainclub.org

Finding the trailhead: From Route 100 in Waterbury Center, turn east onto Howard Avenue. Turn left on Maple Street at the far end of the small village green. Turn right on Loomis Hill Road and travel up the hill approximately 2 miles. At the crest of the hill, the road turns to dirt and bends left, becoming Sweet Road. Continue another 1.5 miles to the parking lot and trailhead on the right (east) side of the road.

The Hike

Mount Hunger is a perennial favorite among hikers in the Stowe area because it is relatively short and has a dazzling view from its open rock summit. It is one of the primary peaks in the Worcester Range, the next ridge east of the Mount Mansfield ridge, and thus is a terrific vantage point for an unobstructed view of the entire Mansfield profile (Adams Apple, Chin, Nose, Forehead). It is also a fun hike because the upper half of the climb has many boulders and ledges to scramble up.

There are several ways to approach the summit of Mount Hunger. The Waterbury Trail (blue blazes) is both the shortest and the most vertical route. It starts out in open woods, strewn with mossy boulders. The footing is excellent, with many rock steps laid into the path by the Vermont Youth Conservation Corps. The trail climbs moderately at first, with intermittent flat sections.

There might be a number of stream crossings if the weather has been wet, but most dry up without consistent rain, except for a rocky cascade at 1.1 miles. The trail

Enjoying the reward on the summit of Mount Hunger. MARK AIKEN

crosses the stream, then turns left, following the left bank. Over the next rise, the trail bears right back across the stream between the upper and lower portion of the falls. The waterfall is often no more than a trickle, but there is always some water in the pool to the left of the crossing.

From here the trail becomes progressively rockier and steeper, though there is a brief reprieve through a patch of ferns and hobblebushes. Hobblebushes are a native shrub with broad leaves. They have large clusters of white flowers in mid-spring and then showy red berries, which are not edible, by midsummer.

The trail continues through a birch grove that still shows evidence of damage caused over two decades ago from a severe ice storm. The damage created a break in the forest canopy that still exists. The first of several short rock walls is just around the bend. Angled cracks and narrow rock shelves provide adequate footing and handholds.

At 2.0 miles the trail to White Rock departs to the right. From here it is a short scramble to the summit of Hunger Mountain.

At 2.2 miles the trail reaches the summit, a bare rock hump with a 360-degree view, but it is tough to take your eyes off Mount Mansfield and Camel's Hump, which dominate the skyline to the east beyond the Waterbury reservoir. The summit is treeless but is not considered a true alpine zone, which is generally above an elevation of

Mount Hunger via the Waterbury Trail

4,000 feet in New England. Instead, it is considered subalpine. Despite this nuance, take care to stay on the rock and off the fragile vegetation.

Return by the same route.

Miles and Directions

0.0 Start at the trailhead for the Waterbury Trail.

1.1 Cross a stream by a rocky cascade.

2.0 The trail to White Rock departs to the right. This optional side-hike adds 1.2 miles round-trip (see sidebar).

2.2 SUMMIT! Return by the same route.

4.4 Arrive back at the trailhead.

PEAK-BAGGER'S BONUS

White Rock Mountain is the rocky, craggy summit just south of Mount Hunger. After summiting Hunger, the connector to White Rock Mountain (0.2 mile below the summit) adds 1.2 miles out and back to your total trip. The path descends for 0.3 mile before ascending toward the summit area of White Rock. At 0.5 mile break out of the heavy canopy onto platforms of slabby schist. Look for blue blazes on the rock, as few trees grow on this moonscape. At the junction with the Middlesex Trail, stay right and continue over an exciting scramble that takes you to the summit of White Rock Mountain. At the top, you'll find a vista similar to the one on Mount Hunger with one bonus: a view of Hunger. Retrace your steps back to the junction with the Waterbury Trail and descend to the trailhead from there.

28 Stowe Pinnacle

Short hike to an open rock knob with a 360-degree view of north-central Vermont.

General location: Stowe
Distance: 3.2 miles out and back
Hiking time: About 3 hours
Highest point: 2,740 feet
Elevation gain: 1,520 feet
Difficulty: More challenging
When to go: Year-round, except during mud season
Canine compatibility: Dog friendly
Trail surface: Packed dirt, rocks, some easy rocky scrambles

Land status: Public
Trail users: Hikers, snowshoers
Water availability: None
Map: USGS Stowe quad
Special considerations: None
Trail contact: Vermont Department of Forests, Parks and Recreation, (802) 476-0182, www.fpr.vermont.gov; Green Mountain Club, (802) 244-7037, www.greenmountainclub.org

Finding the trailhead: From the center of Stowe village, turn south onto School Street. Bear right (south) onto Stowe Hollow Road, which becomes Upper Hollow Road. The trailhead is on the left (east) side of the road, just past Pinnacle Road. There is overflow parking at Pinnacle Meadows. To reach the overflow lot, continue past the Pinnacle Trailhead parking. Take a right on Upper Pinnacle Road, then go straight on Pinnacle Heights Road—a total of 1.4 miles past the trailhead. A double-track leads from the parking area to Pinnacle Meadows and then connects with the main trail.

The Hike

With its impressive summit views, Stowe Pinnacle provides a huge reward for a relatively small effort. It is a favorite among Stowe locals looking for some exercise to a mountaintop destination without a full-day commitment. Located in C. C. Putnam State Forest, the Stowe Pinnacle Trail (blue blazes) is closed during mud season, April 15 to Memorial Day. Most of the hike, until the very end, is shaded, which makes it a good choice on a warm summer day.

The route begins at the back of the trailhead parking lot, traversing a meadow of wildflowers and heading directly toward the mountain. As it approaches the woods, the trail crosses a muddy area on several lengths of puncheons.

At about 0.3 mile the trail passes a giant rock cairn on top of a small boulder. It is a tradition for all who pass to add a stone to the cairn. The trail is wide and strewn with rocks, so it is easy to find one.

After the cairn the trail becomes fairly steep. Eventually it bends to the left and levels off, passing a sapling tepee. It then bends back to the right and begins climbing again.

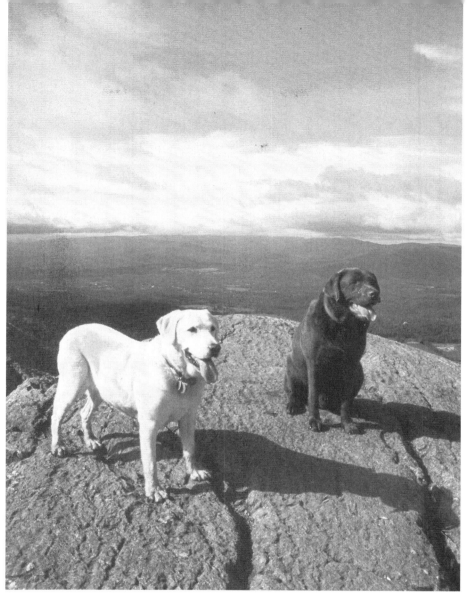

Labs enjoying the view from Stowe Pinnacle. LISA BALLARD

At 0.8 mile the trail reaches a couple of switchbacks and then some muddy stone steps, a welcome aid on the sustained climb. At the top of the first series of steps, the path turns to steplike slab, then back to more-real steps. This pattern continues up the steep slope until the trail reaches a height of land at 1.2 miles, where a spur trail departs to the left to a lookout.

The lookout is a worthwhile spot to catch your breath. You can see the entire Mount Mansfield ridge to the west, the Waterbury reservoir and Sugarbush ski area to the south (far left), and the village of Stowe to the north (right).

Stowe Pinnacle

C. C. PUTNAM
STATE FOREST

Skyline Trail

Stowe
Pinnacle

Stowe Pinnacle Trail

Pinnacle Road

28

Upper Hollow Road

Stowe Hollow Road

School Street

To Morrisville

Main Street

100

To Waterbury

N

0   Kilometer   0.5

0   0.5
Mile

The pitch eases above the lookout. The trail bends right, descending at first, then angling upward across a rooted sidehill. It becomes steep again for a short way as it circles around the north side of the summit. At 1.4 miles the trail reaches the junction with the Skyline Trail. The Skyline Trail, which traverses the Worcester Range to Mount Hunger, departs to the left (southeast). Bear right, climbing through a pine grove, and then cross a long stretch of slab framed by scrub trees.

You then break from the trees and reach the summit at 1.6 miles. Stowe Pinnacle is accurately named. Its summit is literally a pinnacle of bedrock, giving a 360-degree view. The long views, past Mount Elmore to the north, Mount Mansfield to the west, and Sugarbush to the south, are impressive. The view to the east is less expansive, blocked by the wooded Worcester Range.

Return by the same route.

Miles and Directions

0.0 Start at the trailhead for the Stowe Pinnacle Trail.

0.3 Pass a giant cairn on top of a small boulder.

0.8 Climb through switchbacks and then up a series of stone steps.

1.2 VIEWPOINT! Return to the main trail and continue to ascend, though less steeply now.

1.4 Bear right at the junction with the Skyline Trail, continuing on the Stowe Pinnacle Trail.

1.6 SUMMIT! Return by the same route.

3.2 Arrive back at the trailhead.

29 Mount Elmore and Balanced Rock Loop

A popular family hike to a fire tower with a 360-degree view and then to a large boulder that seems to defy gravity.

General location: Elmore
Distance: 3.9-mile lollipop
Hiking time: About 3.5 hours
Highest point: 2,608 feet
Elevation gain: 1,450 feet
Difficulty: More challenging
When to go: Year-round, except during mud season
Canine compatibility: Dog friendly. Dogs must have proof of current rabies vaccination to enter Elmore State Park. They are not allowed at the lake area. Leash must be under 10 feet long. Do not take dogs up the fire tower.

Trail surface: Packed dirt, rocks, some rocky and ledgy scrambles
Land status: Public
Trail users: Hikers, snowshoers
Water availability: Unreliable
Map: USGS Hyde Park quad
Special considerations: A small fee is charged to enter Elmore State Park.
Trail contact: Elmore State Park, (802) 888-2982, https://vtstateparks.com/elmore.html; Vermont Department of Forests, Parks and Recreation, (802) 476-0182, www.fpr.vermont.gov; Green Mountain Club, (802) 244-7037, www.greenmountainclub.org

Finding the trailhead: From the junction of Routes 100 and 12 in Morrisville, take Route 12 south to Elmore State Park. The entrance to the park is on the west side of the road just before Lake Elmore. From the tollbooth at the entrance to the state park, follow the road for 0.5 mile to the trailhead. There is an old chimney stack where a cabin used to stand and picnic tables in the woods near the trailhead parking area.

The Hike

The Worcester Range lies across the Stowe/Waterbury valley to the east of the towering Mount Mansfield ridge. Mount Elmore is the lowest peak in the Worcester Range, but also one of the more prominent and more hiked due to its position at the northern end of the range and its fire tower on top.

From the parking area, follow the Fire Tower Trail (not the Nature Trail). The route starts uphill on a fire road dotted with blue Catamount Ski Trail markers. If the gate is closed, walk around it, passing the stone chimney on the right in the woods and another chimney column on the left. At 0.2 mile the Ridge Trail exits to the right. You'll close your loop here later.

At 0.5 mile, at the end of the fire road, the Catamount Trail continues straight ahead. Take a sharp right (northwest) up stone steps and continue uphill on a single-track. Look for blue blazes now, instead of the plastic Catamount Trail markers.

The fire tower on Mount Elmore. MARK AIKEN

The trail parallels a brook along a fairly steep but smooth grade. The incline eases somewhat as the trail swings sharply right, and then continues climbing up stone steps. From here it winds up the hillside, gaining altitude in waves.

At 1.4 miles you reach a spur to a lookout on the left. The lookout is the site of the old fire-watcher's cabin. All that remains is the stone chimney and a rusty stove. The view, mainly to the east over Lake Elmore, stretches as far as Mount Washington in New Hampshire on a clear day. This is a nice destination in its own right, three-quarters of the way to the summit.

To continue to the fire tower, return to the main trail, climbing on more rugged, vertical terrain. After the short scramble, the trail levels off and arrives at a T. Turn left (south) and go just a few paces to reach the fire tower at 1.7 miles. The tower is exceptionally tall and worth the climb. The view is phenomenal considering the short hike, with Mount Mansfield dominant to the west. Jay Peak and several peaks in southern Quebec fill the northern horizon. The Presidential Range, the Franconia Ridge, and Mount Moosilauke, all in New Hampshire's White Mountains, poke up along the eastern skyline. The rest of the Worcester Range and the main spine of the Green Mountains lie to the south.

To continue to Balanced Rock, return to the T and head north, traversing the upper ridge of the mountain. You're now on the Ridge Trail, which was rebuilt and extended by state trail crews in 2012.

The trail is flat at first and then downhill, and the terrain is mossy, coniferous, and green, as one would imagine the home of elves, fairies, and trolls. It passes two lookouts, the first with a view of Mount Mansfield and the second overlooking Lake Elmore.

Arrive at Balanced Rock at 2.1 miles. As the name implies, Balanced Rock is a large boulder, about 20 feet long and 6 feet high, perched on a rock outcropping. It seems to defy gravity. Push it as hard as you like. It will not budge.

After pondering Balanced Rock, continue along the Ridge Trail, which descends gently. For all of the scrambling and rocks on the way up, the way down is mostly mellow, packed with soft dirt.

At 3.0 miles descend over two wooden stairways, built over a pitch that pales in comparison to some of the rocky uphill scrambles before the fire tower. A short way later, at 3.2 miles, you cross a bridge over a streambed. To the left, the stream spills into a beaver pond. Just past the bridge, there's a faint spur that leads you past several beaver dams, natural wonders of engineering and determination.

The trail itself is a fine example of human engineering. Just after the beaver dams, you'll come to switchbacks, a modern solution to a major washout of the old trail. State park crews plan to continue to adjust the route here in order to create a trail that sheds water more efficiently, so expect further changes in the coming years.

After crossing another bridge over a streambed, the Ridge Trail ends at the Catamount Trail at 3.6 miles. Turn left and follow the Catamount Trail to the parking area at 3.9 miles.

Mount Elmore and Balanced Rock Loop

Miles and Directions

0.0 Start at the trailhead for the Fire Tower Trail, heading uphill on a fire road.

0.5 Turn sharply right at the end of the fire road onto the Mount Elmore Trail.

1.4 Pass a short spur to the site of the former fire-watcher's cabin.

1.7 FIRE TOWER! Turn left and traverse the summit ridge to the north.

2.1 BALANCING ROCK! Continue on the Ridge Trail.

3.2 Pass a beaver pond and several beaver dams.

3.6 Turn left onto the Catamount Trail.

3.9 Arrive back at the trailhead.

30 Mount Mansfield: The Forehead via the Butler Lodge Trail–Maple Ridge Loop

Interesting climb with many ladders and rocky scrambles to the "Forehead" on Mount Mansfield's summit ridge, followed by a dramatic descent along an open alpine buttress on the western side of Vermont's tallest peak.

General location: Underhill Center
Distance: 6.4-mile loop
Hiking time: About 6 hours
Highest point: 3,940 feet
Elevation gain: 2,515 feet
Difficulty: Very strenuous (due to elevation gain)
When to go: Year-round, except during mud season
Canine compatibility: Not dog friendly due to many ladders and rock "chimneys"

Trail surface: Dirt, rocks, ledges, ladders
Land status: Public
Trail users: Hikers, snowshoers, skiers
Water availability: Unreliable streams by the trail, reliable water near Butler Lodge
Map: USGS Mount Mansfield quad
Special considerations: None
Trail contact: Vermont Department of Forests, Parks and Recreation, (802) 879-8329, www.fpr.vermont.gov; Green Mountain Club, (802) 244-7037, www.greenmountainclub.org

Finding the trailhead: From the junction of Routes 15 and 128 in Essex Center, take Route 15 north for 6.5 miles, through Jericho to Underhill Flats. Turn right (east) on River Road and go 2.7 miles to Underhill Center. At the general store in Underhill Center, bear left (northeast) on Pleasant Valley Road. Go 1.5 miles and then bear right (east) on Stevensville Road (aka Maple Leaf Road). Go another mile. The road ends at the trailhead parking area.

The Hike

Mount Mansfield is the tallest mountain in Vermont and among the most spectacular to hike. The profile of the 2-mile summit ridge resembles the face of a man looking skyward. The prominent points of the ridge are commonly known from south to north as the Forehead, the Nose, the Upper Lip, the Lower Lip, the Chin, and the Adams Apple. The Chin (4,393 feet) is the true summit. The loop hike described here takes you to the Forehead at the other end of the ridge. Though you will miss the chance to bag the peak, you will not feel disappointed after the invigorating scramble up ladders and ledges and the incredible views to the west during the long descent to tree line.

From the trailhead sign in the parking lot, walk up the dirt road to the left. Do not take the Nebraska Notch Trail, which is a footpath. Walk around the metal gate (not over the bridge), following the hiking trail sign. The forest road has a broad edge laden with ferns and wildflowers. After a short way, turn left (east) off the road onto the Frost Trail (blue blazes). Almost immediately, you will come to a fork. Bear right onto the Butler Lodge Trail.

Maple Ridge on Mount Mansfield. LISA BALLARD

The trail climbs steadily through hardwoods. At about 1.2 miles it becomes rockier and more eroded. Rock steps aid the ascent a little higher up the slope.

At 1.6 miles the trail reaches a short, four-rung ladder up a low rock wall, though it may be easier to climb up the left side of the rock if the ladder is slippery. From here the trail passes over more sections of slab, and the forest turns to fir trees.

At 1.8 miles the trail passes Wallace Cutoff, arriving at Butler Lodge. Butler Lodge is a small rustic cabin, typical of "lodges" on the Long Trail (LT). This one sleeps up to fourteen. There is also a water source and a privy. Space is available on a first-come, first-served basis, and a small overnight fee might be collected if a caretaker from the Green Mountain Club stops by.

From Butler Lodge, return to the junction of the Butler Lodge Trail and the Wallace Cutoff. Turn left (east) on the Wallace Cutoff, heading toward the LT. The path comes to another ladder, this time up a rock slab under dead tree roots. From here it winds up stone steps and then becomes smoother until the Wallace Cutoff ends at the LT.

At 1.9 miles turn left on the LT–North (white blazes), crossing puncheons and heading upward again. The trail soon levels off, winding through the boreal forest. It heads up again over slab, squeezing between a giant glacial erratic (boulder) on the right and a wall of rock on the left, and then comes to the junction with the bad-weather bypass.

Bear left, remaining on the LT–North. The trail ascends a rock crack as it crests a hump of rock, then drops down to a third ladder. The climb gets more and more interesting as you go around and over rocks, then up yet another ladder hanging on a rock wall. At the top of this ladder, you can see Maple Ridge ahead, which is the way down.

The trail rounds a corner, traverses a catwalk, and then scrambles up more rock. A view of Dewey Mountain and Bolton Mountain lies behind you. After climbing three more ladders, the trail enters the alpine zone. The trees shrink away, leaving wild blueberries along the slab footpath.

At 2.8 miles the trail crests at the Forehead and the junction with the Maple Ridge Trail (blue blazes). This is the highest point of the hike, and the panorama is breathtaking. To the west, Lake Champlain glistens in the sunlight, framed by the Adirondacks on the horizon. Camel's Hump and the tall spine of the Green Mountains travel to the southern horizon. To the north and east, the hulk of Mount Mansfield looms large above you.

The Maple Ridge Trail heads back down the western side of the mountain slightly north of the route you just took up. Maple Ridge is a broad buttress, one of two open rock ridges that head down the mountain from this side. The other, Sunset Ridge, is a little farther north between the Chin and the Nose. The descent is relatively steep until the trail reaches the junction with the Wampahoofus Trail, which departs to the southeast back to Butler Lodge.

Mount Mansfield: The Forehead via the Butler Lodge Trail–Maple Ridge Loop

0   Kilometer   1

0   Mile   1

N

Sterling Pond

Elephant's Head
Cliff

Sterling Pond Trail

Spruce Peak
1,012 m.
3,320 ft.

Hell Brook Trail

The Chin
1,339 m.
4,393 ft.

Adams
Apple

Spruce Peak
Ski Area

Smugglers'
Notch

Elephant's Head
Trail/ Long Trail

Cantilever
Rock

Sunset Ridge Trail

Taft Lodge

Long Trail

Barnes Loop
Trail

UNDERHILL
STATE PARK

Laura Cowles Trail

M
O
U
N
T

M
A
N
S
F
I
E
L
D

Barnes Camp

Eagles
Cut Trail

Long Trail

CCC Road

Stowe
Ski Area

Mountain
Road

The Nose

108

To Underhill
Center

Maple Ridge

Maple Ridge Trail

The Forehead

To Stowe

Butler Lodge

Frost Trail

Toll Road

Stevensville
Road

Butler Lodge Trail

Long Trail

30

Nebraska
Notch Trail

Continue downhill on the Maple Ridge Trail. Though still on rock slab, some side-angled, the incline becomes more moderate. Lake Champlain lies ahead the entire time.

After jumping a small gap in the rock, the trail winds around several rock outcroppings. Watch the blue blazes carefully in this section to stay on the trail, as it is easy to get distracted by the many ledges and lookout points. Eventually the trail comes to a tall ledge, which is easier to descend on the right side or via a diagonal crack.

At 3.6 miles a second trail, the Rock Garden Trail, departs to the left, also back to Butler Lodge. Bear right, continuing on the Maple Ridge Trail. The trail continues over open rock, offering long views as it continues downhill through interesting miniature chasms and over more rock outcroppings.

At 3.9 miles the Maple Ridge Trail comes to a junction with the Frost Trail. Turn left onto the Frost Trail. Grass and ferns begin to line the trail, and then it finally reenters the tree line. The trail turns to dirt, and white birches soon work their way into the forest mix.

There is a stream crossing just before you close the loop at 6.2 miles. Return to the trailhead at 6.4 miles.

Miles and Directions

0.0 Start by taking the dirt road to the left (not the footpath to Nebraska Notch).

0.1 Turn left (east) onto the Frost Trail. Immediately bear right onto the Butler Lodge Trail.

1.6 Climb the first of several ladders.

1.8 BUTLER LODGE! Take the Wallace Cutoff from the lodge toward the LT.

1.9 Turn left on the LT–North.

2.8 THE FOREHEAD! Descend via the Maple Ridge Trail along the open rock ridge.

3.6 At the junction with the Rock Garden Trail, bear right, remaining on the Maple Ridge Trail.

3.9 Turn left onto the Frost Trail.

6.2 Close the loop at the junction with the Butler Lodge Trail.

6.4 Arrive back at the trailhead.

31 Mount Mansfield via the Sunset Ridge Trail

A look at gravity-defying Cantilever Rock and then an ascent to the summit of the tallest mountain in Vermont via a dramatic alpine ridge.

General location: Underhill State Park
Distance: 6.8 miles out and back, including 0.2 mile to Cantilever Rock
Hiking time: About 6 hours
Highest point: 4,393 feet
Elevation gain: 2,550 feet
Difficulty: Very strenuous (due to elevation gain)
When to go: Year-round, except during mud season
Canine compatibility: Dog friendly, though some challenging ledgy areas. Dogs must be on leashes no longer than 10 feet in the state park campground. Proof of rabies vaccination is required to enter the state park. Puppies too young for a vaccination will not be admitted. In the alpine zone (above tree line), dogs must be on a leash no longer than 5 feet and must stay on the trail. Dogs may be off leash, under voice control, above the campground and below tree line.
Trail surface: Dirt, rocks, rocky slab, ledges requiring some scrambling
Land status: Public
Nearest amenities: Underhill Center
Trail users: Hikers, snowshoers, skiers
Water availability: Unreliable
Map: USGS Mount Mansfield quad
Special considerations: There is a day-use fee to enter Underhill State Park.
Trail contact: Mid-May to mid-October, Underhill State Park, (802) 899-3022, www.vtstate parks.com or, off-season, Vermont Department of Forests, Parks and Recreation, (802) 879-8329, www.fpr.vermont.gov; Green Mountain Club, (802) 244-7037, www.greenmountain club.org

Finding the trailhead: From the junction of Routes 15 and 128 in Essex Center, take Route 15 north for 6.5 miles, through Jericho to Underhill Flats. Turn right (east) onto River Road, which bends to the left and becomes Pleasant Valley Road in Underhill Center. Turn right onto Mountain Road, which ends at Underhill State Park. The trailhead is technically 1 mile up the dirt road from the far end of the parking lot, but this is the farthest you can drive.

The Hike

Just the fact that Mount Mansfield is the tallest peak in Vermont makes it a magnet for hikers. About 40,000 people make it to the top of this landmark each year, though they are spread out among a number of different routes along every side of the mountain. A toll road from the Stowe Mountain Resort doubles as a ski trail during the winter. It allows people to drive within a mile of the summit, giving all but the weakest hikers a chance to reach the top of this famous peak. The gondola from the ski area also brings people up to the ridge in the summertime, but it is still a demanding and cliffy 2 miles to the summit from the top of the gondola. The Long Trail (LT) traverses the summit ridge, allowing ascents from both the north and the south. And these are just a sampling of the ways to reach the summit of this iconic peak.

View toward the Forehead (south) from the Chin of Mount Mansfield. LISA BALLARD

The Sunset Ridge Trail (blue blazes), one of the routes from the west, is popular because much of it is above tree line. It also has a unique side attraction called Cantilever Rock, a huge narrow boulder that extends 25 feet from a cliff, parallel to the ground, seeming to defy gravity.

The route begins in Underhill State Park in the 34,000-acre Mount Mansfield State Forest. The state park has eleven tent sites, six lean-tos, and restrooms with cold water and flush toilets, but no showers. Head up the dirt road at the end of the parking lot. The road is closed to traffic, but if you prefer a more trail-like path, take the Eagles Cut Trail (blue blazes), which starts at the upper parking lot. Both the road and the trail lead to the Sunset Ridge Trail, crisscrossing each other, until the trail merges with the road at 0.3 mile.

At 1.0 mile the route comes to a sign-in box and the start of the Sunset Ridge Trail. The CCC road, popular with backcountry skiers, heads to the right. Ignore this and instead bear left into the woods, where you'll immediately cross over three bridges.

The trail comes to the lower junction with the Laura Cowles Trail at 1.1 miles. Bear left over another bridge to stay on the Sunset Ridge Trail.

After a couple more bridges, the trail starts to climb over slab, scattered rocks, and rock steps, passing over even more bridges and by a large boulder. The trail eventually comes to the first of several steeper sections of slab. From the top of it, turn around for your first view of Camel's Hump in the distance.

Mount Mansfield via the Sunset Ridge Trail

To Jefferssonville

Smugglers' Notch
Ski Area

108

Sterling
Pond

Snuffy's Ski Trail/
Long Trail

Sterling Pond
Shelter

Sterling Pond Trail

Long Trail

Elephant's Head
Cliff

Elephant's
Head Trail

Hell Brook Trail

Spruce Peak
1,012 m.
3,320 ft.

West Branch Waterbury River

The Chin
1,339 m.
4,393 ft.

Adams
Apple

Spruce Peak
Ski Area

Smugglers'
Notch

Elephant's Head Trail/
Long Trail

Cantilever
Rock

Sunset Ridge Trail

Taft Lodge

UNDERHILL
STATE PARK

Laura Cowles Trail

M O U N T   M A N S F I E L D

Long Trail

Barnes Loop
Trail

Eagles
Cut Trail

CCC Road

Long Trail

Barnes Camp

31

Stowe
Ski Area

Mountain
Road

The Nose

To Underhill
Center

Maple Ridge

Maple Ridge Trail

The Forehead

Butler Lodge

Toll Road

108

Frost Trail

Butler Lodge Trail

Long Trail

To Stowe

At 1.8 miles the spur to Cantilever Rock departs to the left. Only 0.1 mile away, it is worth the short side trip, either on the way up or on the way down. Cantilever Rock looks like a rock gangplank, protruding far into the air above a tall cliff at a 90-degree angle to the ground. It was left in its seemingly impossible position when the continental glaciers receded at the end of the last ice age. Cantilever Rock seems to defy gravity when viewed from below.

Return to the main trail and continue up through ferns and birches. The trail passes a chasm between three large boulders, which were likely one mammoth boulder long ago. Today a streamlet flows out of the gap in the rocks.

A few minutes later, the trail reaches another boulder formation, this time with a small cave. A streamlet flows out of the cave too. You can walk through it or go around on the main trail to keep your feet dry.

Several small overhangs will catch your eye as the trail winds up through the rock then breaks out on a rocky outcropping. Technically, the alpine zone begins here. The upper Sunset Ridge and the Chin are visible above you to the left (northeast). Camel's Hump dominates the view to the right (south), and the Champlain Valley spreads out before you to the west.

Continue up the steep slab. For the rest of the route, the vistas are endless, but it is tough to take your eyes off the Chin, the distinct rocky knob that looms above. First blueberries and then wild cranberries, also called lingonberries, carpet the rocks between the scrub spruce trees.

At the sign for the Chin Natural Area, the trail bends to the right, traversing toward the Nose, and then comes to a junction with the upper end of the Laura Cowles Trail. Bear left (uphill).

At 3.2 miles the Sunset Ridge Trail ends at the summit ridge, where it meets the Long Trail (white blazes). Turn left onto the LT–North, crossing over puncheons and continuing toward the summit. Take care to step only on rock rather than the fragile alpine plants.

The advantage of being on the highest peak in Vermont is an expansive, unobstructed view in all directions. On a clear day, you can see all the way to Mount Royale in Montreal to the north, Whiteface Mountain and the Adirondacks across Lake Champlain to the west, Camel's Hump and the main spine of the Green Mountains to the south, and the Worcester Range (close) and the White Mountains in New Hampshire (far) to the east.

Return by the same route.

Miles and Directions

0.0 Begin on the dirt road at the end of the parking lot or on the Eagles Cut Trail.

0.3 The Eagles Cut Trail merges onto the dirt road.

1.0 Bear left (north) off the dirt road onto the Sunset Ridge Trail.

1.1 Bear left at the junction with the Laura Cowles Trail, continuing on the Sunset Ridge Trail.

1.8 Turn left onto the spur to Cantilever Rock.

1.9 CANTILEVER ROCK! Retrace your steps back to the Sunset Ridge Trail.

2.0 Turn left, continuing to climb up the Sunset Ridge Trail.

3.2 The Sunset Ridge Trail ends at the LT. Turn left on the LT–North.

3.4 SUMMIT! You've reached the Chin. Return by the same route.

6.8 Arrive back at the trailhead.

32 Mount Mansfield via the Long Trail-South

Steady, steep climb past Taft Lodge, with magnificent views and fun rocky scrambles on the way to the top of the tallest peak in Vermont.

General location: Smugglers' Notch
Distance: 4.6 miles out and back
Hiking time: About 5 hours
Highest point: 4,393 feet
Elevation gain: 2,800 feet
Difficulty: Very strenuous (due to elevation gain)
When to go: Year-round, except during mud season
Canine compatibility: Questionable due to many rock "walls" and ledges

Trail surface: Dirt, rocks, ledges that require scrambling
Land status: Public
Nearest amenities: Stowe or Jeffersonville
Trail users: Hikers, snowshoers, skiers
Water availability: Unreliable
Map: USGS Mount Mansfield quad
Special considerations: None
Trail contact: Green Mountain Club, (802) 244-7037, www.greenmountainclub.org

Finding the trailhead: From the junction of Routes 100 and 108 in the center of Stowe, turn onto Route 108 north. Go 8.1 miles through the ski area and into Smugglers' Notch. From Jeffersonville, take Route 108 south for 9.4 miles. (*Note:* Route 108 through Smugglers' Notch is not open during the winter.) Park on the west side of the road in the designated parking area, then walk back 50 yards to the trailhead for the Long Trail (LT)–South, which is on the opposite side of Route 108.

The Hike

This hike sounds easy due to its low mileage, but don't be fooled. It climbs 2,800 vertical feet in only 2.3 miles. You should be comfortable scrambling up multiple short rock chimneys and ledgy areas before taking on this one. Save it for a dry day, as the upper part of the hike can be treacherous if the rocks are wet, and the summit ridge is completely exposed to the weather. That said, the top of Mount Mansfield is the top of Vermont, with views stretching into neighboring New Hampshire, New York, and Quebec on a clear day. This route is the most popular way to hike to the summit from the Stowe side of the mountain.

Take the LT–South (white blazes) into the woods. It is a smooth climb at first through hardwoods. Soon you can hear a stream to your left through the trees. The trail ascends log steps parallel to the stream, though you cannot see it.

At 0.3 mile the trail bends right (northwest), then climbs more steeply up big rock steps. Soon it levels off again, crossing a streamlet, then winds upward over smaller steps, gaining noticeable altitude. It sags briefly, crosses another streamlet, and then continues to climb. The trail becomes rockier with more mini-stream crossings,

View from a high shoulder of Mount Mansfield. LISA BALLARD

though many of these trickles dry up. Yellow and paper birches are noticeable throughout the forest, evidence of the higher elevation.

After more stone steps and yet another streamlet across the path, a view to the northeast teases you through the trees at 0.8 mile. The rocky trail continues its steady climb, flattening out only on one short traverse. Though you are still under the canopy, the trees are thinning. You can glimpse the snowmaking pond (aka Peregrine Lake) at the base of Spruce Peak, part of the Stowe Mountain Resort.

At 1.0 mile the trail climbs a shallow ledge, then bends right (west) over a section of sidehill slab and up a short washout. The incline mellows as you enter a grove of hemlocks, signaling your entrance into the boreal zone. The relief is brief. The eroded trail soon winds upward and becomes rocky rubble underfoot.

After a particularly long, steep ascent up slab and ledge, you are rewarded with the first open view at 1.4 miles. Mountains trail away to the northeast from Madonna Peak on the opposite side of Smugglers' Notch. From here the trail flattens as it traverses toward the summit ridge, which towers like a wall in front of you.

At 1.6 miles you can see the towers on top of the Forehead, one of the subpeaks of Mount Mansfield, and the famous Nosedive ski trail, which falls off a shoulder of the summit ridge like a bright green shawl during the summer.

The trail bends north, passing the junction with the Hell Brook Cutoff, which departs to the right (east). At 1.7 miles it comes to a three-way intersection. The path on the left goes to Taft Lodge. The right one goes to the lodge's outhouse, and the center path continues to the summit.

Taft Lodge sits at an elevation of 3,650 feet. The original cabin was built in 1920, then rebuilt in 1996. As with all of the cabins and shelters on the Long Trail, it is available on a first-come, first-served basis and is maintained by the Green Mountain Club. A small overnight fee may be charged. Tent camping is not allowed near the cabin.

Shortly after leaving Taft Lodge, the trail comes to the junction with the Profanity Trail, which departs to the left (west). For through-hikers on the LT, this is the summit bypass in case of bad weather. For the day hike described here, if the weather is bad, this is your turnaround point. It is dangerous to go above tree line in stormy weather.

As you near the alpine zone, the sky appears overhead as you pass through short spruce trees and alpine "grasses." You can see the ski trails and the summit ridge. After a few more steps, the Worcester Range, the next range to the east, and New Hampshire's White Mountains, on the eastern horizon, come into view.

At 2.0 miles the trail comes to a three-way junction with the Hell Brook Trail and the Adams Apple Trail. The Adams Apple, which marks the northern end of the Mount Mansfield ridge, is the hump above you to the right. Turn left, continuing on the LT–South toward the Chin.

The trail crosses puncheons, then climbs again up open slab to a vertical rock crack. From here, it is a fun scramble up another rock chimney and many ledges. The route levels off for the last 100 yards to the summit, where views of the Adirondacks (west) and White Mountains (east) will make your jaw drop.

Return by the same route.

Miles and Directions

0.0 Start at the trailhead for the LT-South.

0.3 Bend right (northwest) and climb stone steps.

1.0 Cross sidehill slab and a small washout, entering the boreal zone.

1.4 First view of Madonna Peak to the north.

1.6 View of the towers on the Forehead and the Nosedive ski trail.

1.7 TAFT LODGE! Continue on the LT-South toward the summit.

2.0 At the three-way junction with the Hell Brook Trail and the Adams Apple Trail, turn left, continuing on the LT-South.

2.3 SUMMIT! Return by the same route.

4.6 Arrive back at the trailhead.

33 Elephant's Head Cliff–Sterling Pond Loop

A steep ascent out of a narrow notch to a cliff-top lookout, then a moderate ascent to a scenic subalpine pond with views of Mount Mansfield along much of the route.

General location: Smugglers' Notch
Distance: 6.5-mile loop
Hiking time: About 5 hours
Highest point: 3,100 feet
Elevation gain: 1,780 feet
Difficulty: More challenging
When to go: Year-round, except during mud season
Canine compatibility: Questionable due to one ladder at the first slide crossing, the steep stairs on the northern end of pond, and some rough terrain. Only experienced hiking dogs should go on this route.

Trail surface: Dirt, rocks, some rocky scrambles, ladders, slide path crossings
Land status: Public
Nearest amenities: Stowe or Jeffersonville
Trail users: Hikers, snowshoers, skiers
Water availability: Streams, pond, unreliable spring at Sterling Pond shelter
Map: USGS Mount Mansfield quad
Special considerations: None
Trail contact: Green Mountain Club, (802) 244-7037, www.greenmountainclub.org

Finding the trailhead: From the junction of Routes 100 and 108 in Stowe, follow Route 108 (Mountain Road) north for 8.1 miles through the Stowe Mountain Resort and into Smugglers' Notch. The trailhead is on the right (north) side of the road at the Smugglers' Notch Picnic Area. From Jeffersonville, take Route 108 south for 9.4 miles. The picnic area has plenty of parking.
Note: During the winter, the portion of Route 108 through Smugglers' Notch is not plowed. In wintertime, come from Stowe and park at the Barnes Camp lot just past the ski area by the barricade across Route 108. From there, walk the short distance to the picnic area.

The Hike

Smugglers' Notch is a deep, narrow cleft that separates the hulk of Mount Mansfield and a high ridge that includes Spruce Peak and Madonna Peak. Geologists believe the notch was formed by a river that flowed toward Stowe during the last ice age, carving the dramatic cliffs that form its walls.

The name Smugglers' Notch dates back to before the War of 1812, when the notch was used as an illegal trade route with Canada during a trade embargo with the British Commonwealth. The notch was also used during Prohibition to smuggle illegal alcoholic beverages from Canada into Vermont.

This hike takes you up the northern side of Smugglers' Notch, opposite Mount Mansfield, to the top of Elephant's Head Cliff and then to Sterling Pond via the Long Trail (LT)–North (white blazes), also known as the Elephant's Head Trail. It descends via the Sterling Pond Trail, which used to be the LT–North before it was rerouted.

From the parking area, pick up the Barnes Loop Trail (blue blazes) by the restrooms at the southern end of the parking area. The Barnes Loop is relatively new, having been completed in 2018 as part of a larger Smugglers' Notch Long Trail relocation project that took several years. It connects the Long Trail to the historic Barnes Camp, a former logging camp located a mile south on Route 108 that has through the years served as a shelter for hikers, a ski dorm, housing for Green Mountain Club caretakers, and, currently, a visitor center.

After 100 yards on the Barnes Loop Trail, turn left at the intersection onto the LT–North (which follows the same path as the Barnes Loop for a time), then climb the steep ladderlike steps at the edge of the West Branch Waterbury River. The river is more like a shallow brook here (and, indeed, it's also known as Notch Brook). There used to be a footbridge, but it washed away during a spring flood. This is a wet crossing if the water is high. Bear left on the opposite side of the stream onto the LT–North.

The path soon crosses a smaller tributary and then bends right (south), following the stream and the surrounding marshy wetland filled with beaver-cut stumps and heading toward Stowe. The ski trails on Mount Mansfield are visible high to your right.

The trail climbs steeply up the wall of the notch, aided by switchbacks, still heading toward Stowe. The ascent eases briefly after passing a rock wall, then begins a long traverse back to the north. The trail soon climbs persistently again until it passes another rock wall on your right. The route finally mellows as it heads back into the notch.

At 0.4 mile the Barnes Loop goes right. Leave the Loop and continue on the LT–North (white blazes) by staying left. Continue sidehill as the LT–North climbs the notch wall.

At 1.1 miles the trail passes some slabby rock steps. Be sure to glance over your shoulder for views of Mansfield's Chin—Vermont's high point—as you enter a birch glade. Shortly thereafter, the birches give way to fragrant balsam firs as the going steepens on a smooth, soft surface.

At 1.5 miles the trail crosses the narrow lower portion of a landslide that dates back to 1985 and climbs a ladder. After several long switchbacks, it recrosses the slide higher up, heading briefly south. The trail then rounds another elongated switchback and continues on a long traverse back to the north.

You eventually arrive at a highly constructed, yet moss-covered and dilapidated, pyramid-shaped staircase that climbs a large rocky knob partially buried in the mountainside. As you ascend the steps, look across the notch for a spectacular view of Mount Mansfield and its Hell Brook cliff, a vertical rock wall on the opposite side of the notch.

The trail becomes fairly rough now as it ambles along the side of the notch wall, often hanging on the mountainside. But the climb is moderate and rewards with intermittent views of Mount Mansfield.

Sterling Pond with Madonna Peak looming beyond. MARK AIKEN

At 2.3 miles the trail comes to a T. Turn left (west) to take the short spur 0.1 mile to the top of Elephant's Head. (**Note:** The cliff area might be closed if peregrine falcons are nesting.) It is a steep descent to the top of the cliffs and not recommended if snow or ice is on the trail. However, if the rocks are dry, it's worth a look. Directly across from this lofty perch on the opposite side of the notch is a massive rockslide that snakes 1,000 feet down. It fell in the spring of 2020, sending several house-sized boulders all the way to the road. One of the boulders hit a parked car. Return to the junction with the LT, continuing on the LT–North.

The LT crosses a wet area, then climbs in waves, sometimes steeply, to a plateau. It winds through evergreens, which shelter the trail like walls and a roof, then bends left (northeast) and merges with a narrow ski trail, called Snuffy's Trail, at 3.0 miles. Snuffy's Trail, named for a former ski patroller at the Stowe Mountain Resort, comes from the summit of Spruce Peak, another worthwhile 0.2-mile detour. This old, flat ski trail is a connector that, during a good snow year, allows skiers to travel between the Stowe Mountain Resort and the Smugglers' Notch Ski Area. There are unobstructed views from the ski trail into the notch and up to Mount Mansfield's Chin.

Here, the LT–North and Elephant's Head Trail split. You could follow the LT left along Snuffy's Trail, a gravel double-track, to Sterling Pond (and cut 0.7 mile off the route), but this description instead follows the quieter and more scenic Elephant's

Navigating the rocks while circling Sterling Pond on the Elephant's Head. MARK AIKEN

0   Kilometer   1

0   Mile   1

N

To Jeffersonville

Smugglers' Notch
Ski Area

108

Sterling
Pond

Snuffy's Ski Trail/
Long Trail

Sterling Pond
Shelter

Elephant's Head
Cliff

Sterling Pond Trail

Long Trail

Elephant's
Head Trail

Hell Brook Trail

Spruce Peak
1,012 m.
3,320 ft.

West Branch Waterbury River

The Chin
1,339 m.
4,393 ft.

Adams
Apple

Spruce Peak
Ski Area

Cantilever
Rock

Sunset Ridge Trail

Taft Lodge

Smugglers'
Notch

Elephant's Head Trail/
Long Trail

Laura Cowles Trail

Long Trail

33

Barnes Loop
Trail

UNDERHILL
STATE PARK

M O U N T   M A N S F I E L D

Eagles
Cut Trail

Long Trail

Barnes Camp

CCC Road

Mountain
Road
To Underhill
Center

The Nose

Stowe
Ski Area

Maple Ridge

Maple Ridge Trail

The Forehead

Toll Road

108

Frost Trail

Butler Lodge

Butler Lodge Trail

Long Trail

To Stowe

Head Trail around the pond. Cross Snuffy's on the Elephant's Head Trail and descend through the conifers.

At 3.4 miles the trail goes over and through some cave-like rocks, requiring moderate scrambling. Arrive at the southern and far less trafficked tip of the pond at 3.5 miles. Sterling Pond is a kidney-shaped tarn. It is considered a "fragile vegetation area," so stay on the trail to avoid damaging the flora.

The Elephant's Head Trail circumnavigates the pond, passing several small, secluded beach spots. Take advantage of the pond on this end, as solitude is rare on the heavily visited northern end of the pond.

At 3.7 miles the Elephant's Head Trail ends at Sterling Pond Shelter, a wooden lean-to structure, and several tent sites. There is an unreliable spring a few hundred yards beyond the shelter. The LT–North heads right, but follow the LT–South, passing the shelter and continuing along the pond's edge.

At 3.9 miles the trail arrives at the top of the Sterling chairlift, part of the Smugglers' Notch Ski Area. The trail goes directly under the lift's top, archlike tower, alongside its giant concrete hanging counterweight. Several steps beyond, descend a steep wooden staircase above the pond, which leads to a popular lunch spot with summer and fall groups from the Smugglers' Notch Ski Area. Madonna Peak, the highest point of the ski area, overlooks the opposite shoreline.

After enjoying the pond, follow the LT–South/Snuffy's Trail to the junction with the Sterling Pond Trail at 4.1 miles. Bear right (west) on the Sterling Pond Trail. From here it is a steep mile down to the notch road. It is a well-used trail, wet in places and quite rough.

At 5.1 miles the Sterling Pond Trail ends at the notch road and an information booth. You are now on the Jeffersonville side of the notch. Turn left and follow Route 108 back through the notch. It is a pleasant walk, even though it is on a paved road. The road is narrow and winding, with Elephant's Head and other towering cliffs on either side of you. It is especially nice to walk the notch road during the winter, when it is closed to traffic.

Close the loop at your car at 6.5 miles.

Miles and Directions

0.0 Take the LT–North/Barnes Camp Loop from the Smugglers' Notch Picnic Area. Turn left at the first T, crossing the West Branch Waterbury River, and ascend the wall of the notch.

0.4 Bear left on the LT–North.

1.5 Cross an old landslide.

2.3 ELEPHANT'S HEAD CLIFF! Turn right to continue on the LT–North to Sterling Pond.

3.0 Cross Snuffy's Trail, following the Elephant's Head Trail.

3.4 Scramble over cave-like rocks.

3.5 STERLING POND! Continue on the Elephant's Head Trail around the pond.

3.7 SHELTER! Continue around the pond on the LT–South.

3.9 Pass under the top of a ski lift and descend steep stairs to a pondside lunch spot. Follow the LT–South/Snuffy's Trail.

4.1 Turn right on the Sterling Pond Trail.

5.1 Turn left (south) on Route 108 and head through Smugglers' Notch.

6.5 Close the loop at the trailhead at the Smugglers' Notch Picnic Area.

HISTORY OF THE LONG TRAIL AND GREEN MOUNTAIN CLUB

The Long Trail (LT), which runs 270 miles, the entire length of Vermont from the Massachu-setts border to Canada, is the original "through-trail" in North America. It was conceived in 1910 by a hiker named James P. Taylor, while waiting for the clouds to lift from the top of Stratton Mountain, though it would take another twenty years to complete. It was not a solo effort. Shortly after Taylor had the idea for the Long Trail, he gathered a group of twenty-three other passionate hikers in Burlington, Vermont. This led to the formation of the Green Mountain Club (GMC), which is credited with building the LT and which continues to maintain it today.

The LT became the model for the Appalachian Trail (AT), which was proposed eleven years later by Benton MacKaye, a forester and regional planner for the USDA Forest Service, also from atop Stratton Mountain. People considering the AT from start to finish sometimes try the LT first to get a sense of through-hiking. In fact, the southern half of the LT is concurrent with the AT in Vermont.

The LT follows the high ridge of the Green Mountains, over alpine peaks, through quiet woodlands, and past pristine ponds, thus cherry-picking many of the best destinations from a hiking point of view. In addition to the LT itself, there are another 175 miles of trails that access it. Though sections of trail have changed over time due to erosion and access issues, the basic route is unchanged since it was first created.

The member-based Green Mountain Club is not only the primary steward of the LT, overseeing its maintenance, but also its advocate. In addition, the club runs programs that educate people on low-impact and other backcountry skills and publishes books and other references on the LT and its subsidiary trails. The GMC works with the Vermont Department of Forests, Parks and Recreation, the USDA Forest Service, the National Park Service, the Appa-lachian Trail Conservancy, and private landowners to ensure that day hikers and backpackers can continue to enjoy Vermont's backcountry. Most recently, the GMC partnered with several agencies to create the Kingdom Heritage Trail in Vermont's Northeast Kingdom (see Hike 39).

Northern Green Mountains

Johnson to the Canadian Border

34 Devil's Gulch–Ritterbush Pond Loop

A multifaceted loop that passes by two lovely ponds and through a rock tunnel and a lush, deep ravine to a high perch.

General location: Belvidere Corners
Distance: 5.4-mile loop, with a 0.4-mile out-and-back hike through Devil's Gulch
Hiking time: About 3.5 hours
Highest point: 2,100 feet
Elevation gain: 900 feet
Difficulty: Moderate
When to go: Year-round, except during mud season
Canine compatibility: Dog friendly to the ponds only. Devil's Gulch is not dog friendly except for extremely experienced and sure-footed dogs.

Trail surface: Dirt, rocks, stone steps, lots of boulder scrambling
Land status: Public
Nearest amenities: Jeffersonville
Trail users: Hikers, snowshoers
Water availability: Ponds, streams, brooks, spring behind Spruce Ledge Camp
Map: USGS Eden quad
Special considerations: None
Trail contact: Green Mountain Club, (802) 244-7037, www.greenmountainclub.com

Finding the trailhead: From the junction of Routes 100 and 118 in Eden, turn north on Route 118 and go 4.7 miles. Turn right (northeast) at the sign for the Long Trail Access to find the trailhead parking.

The Hike

From the trailhead, take the Long Trail (LT)–South (white blazes) back to Route 118 and cross the road. This spot is called Eden Crossing (elevation 1,137 feet) by through-hikers on the LT. On the opposite side of the road, bear left (east) for about 25 yards along the road. At the white arrow on the tree, turn right (south) into the woods. The trail passes through a northern hardwood forest, traversing a hillside as it gently climbs. At a height of land, it rolls along, sometimes up and sometimes down, until it leaves the plateau and begins a more sustained but gentle descent.

The first mile of the route lacks many distinguishing landmarks other than rolling hills and intermittent views of farmlands through the trees. At 1.0 mile the path descends gently as it parallels a trickling brook.

At 1.7 miles the path comes to a rocky outcropping. Though you are still under the forest canopy, there is a nice view of Ritterbush Pond below you to the south. From here descend, first on steep rocks, then on impressive stone steps, in the direction of the pond. The trail levels off and then runs parallel to the western shoreline, though a distance above it, along the hillside.

At 2.0 miles the LT comes to a junction with the Babcock Trail. To check out Ritterbush Pond, turn left (south) on the Babcock Trail, heading downhill a short way

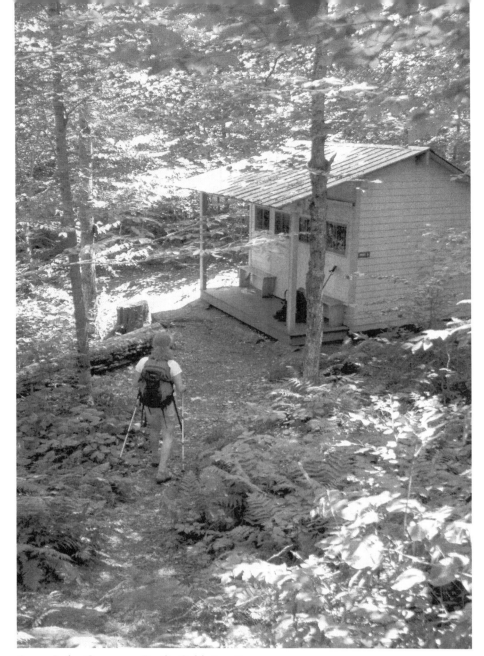

Spruce Ledge Camp near Devil's Gulch. LISA BALLARD

to a dirt road by the edge of the pond. Beavers have turned the saplings into stumps along this corner of the shoreline. There is an excellent view across the pond beyond a small frog pool.

Retrace your steps to the junction and our route. Continue south (left) on the LT–South, passing the junction with the Babcock Trail, which heads away from the

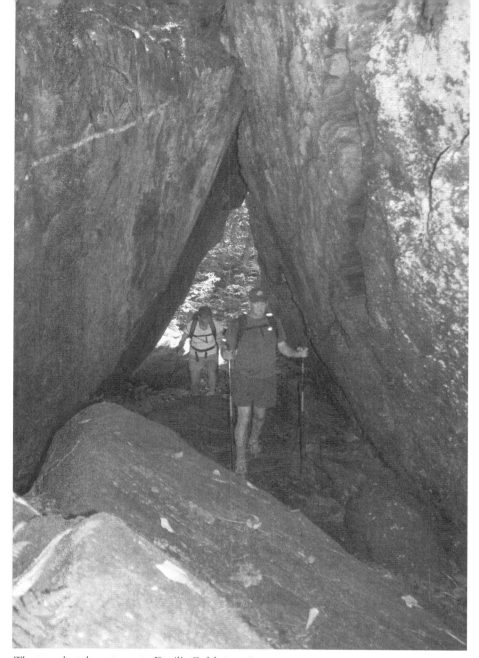

The tunnel at the entrance to Devil's Gulch. LISA BALLARD

pond. This will be your return route. A third of a mile beyond the trail junction, the LT bends right up a short ladder.

At 2.6 miles a sign marks the entrance to Devil's Gulch. Two enormous disc-shaped boulders form an A-frame tunnel, a portal into the otherworldly canyon beyond. It's slow going through Devil's Gulch as you scramble over mossy rocks and marvel at the 175-foot rock walls to either side. It feels like a rain forest, with lush flora and trickles of water welling out of the cliffs and up from the floor of the narrow valley. Devil's Gulch is less than a quarter-mile long, but it is very memorable.

From the opposite end of the gulch, the trail heads uphill parallel to a streamlet. At 2.9 miles it crosses the streamlet and then comes to a junction with the spur trail (blue blazes) to Spruce Ledge Camp, a cabin maintained by the Green Mountain Club that is available on a first-come, first-served basis. Recross the stream, bearing left (east) at the sign, up stone steps toward the cabin. Due to its northern location along a less-traveled section of the LT, Spruce Ledge Camp provides relative solitude even on weekends.

Pass the cabin and picnic table, continuing on the footpath to Devil's Perch, also called Devil's Gulch Lookout on some maps. From the bench, there is a nice view over Ritterbush Pond to Belvidere Mountain. Belvidere is easy to identify due to the fire tower on its summit and the pile of asbestos tailings from an old mine on the right (east) side of the mountain.

After enjoying the view, retrace your steps back through Devil's Gulch to the junction with the Babcock Trail at 4.0 miles. This time, turn left (north) onto the Babcock Trail, heading uphill. It's a steady ascent on a rock-strewn footpath under towering maples.

At 4.6 miles there is a break in the canopy as you reach a height of land. The trail then descends gently as you approach the southern tip of Big Muddy Pond. Big Muddy Pond is long and thin, with a beaver dam at its south end. It doesn't seem very muddy when you look at it from the trail, which runs along the west side of the pond.

Just when you think you'll have to ascend the good-sized hills on the northern end of the pond, the trail bends right (east) around the top of the pond, where you'll see an impressive beaver lodge. Descend via the pond's drainage. At 5.1 miles the route levels off and continues through the lush forest. It reaches Route 118 at 5.4 miles at a different spot than the road crossing near the trailhead.

Cross the road and then take the Babcock Trail Extension (blue blazes) downhill. The grassy trail ends at a dirt road. Turn right (east) on the road, then turn right again back into the woods. Traverse through a pine grove, crossing a series of puncheons. From here the trail climbs gently into a mixed forest with a carpet of ferns, reaching your car at 5.8 miles.

Miles and Directions

0.0 Start by crossing Route 118 and head into the woods on the LT-South. Descend gently alongside a trickling brook.

1.7 VIEW! See Ritterbush Pond from a rocky outcropping, then descend toward the pond.

2.0 POND! Turn left on the Babcock Trail at a four-way intersection to the water's edge, then return to the intersection and continue on the LT-South.

2.6 TUNNEL! Enter Devil's Gulch through an A-frame boulder tunnel.

Devil's Gulch–Ritterbush Pond Loop

Kilometers

Miles

N

Tillotson Peak
927 m.
3,040 ft.

Tillotson
Camp

Frank Post Trail

Mines Road

Long Trail

Forester Trail

Tillotson Road

Long Trail

Belvidere Mountain
1,024 m.
3,360 ft.

Belvidere
Pond

P

P 34

Belvidere
Corners

Big
Muddy
Pond

Babcock Trail

Long Trail

Ritterbush
Lookout

To Eden Mills

Devil's Gulch

Ritterbush Pond

Devil's Gulch
Lookout

Spruce
Lodge

Long Trail

To Eden

2.9 VIEW! Turn left onto a spur trail, passing Spruce Ledge Camp on your way to Devil's Perch for a view of Mount Belvidere. Return through Devil's Gulch to the intersection with the Babcock Trail.

4.0 Return to the junction of the LT and Babcock Trail. Turn left on the Babcock Trail, heading uphill.

4.6 Approach Big Muddy Pond, then traverse above its western shoreline before descending through a drainage on its northern end.

5.1 Pass through a lush, mixed forest.

5.4 Recross Route 118 (different spot), then take the Babcock Trail Extension.

5.8 Close the loop back at your car.

35 Belvidere Mountain Loop

A peaceful loop hike past a large beaver pond and Tillotson Camp to a 50-foot fire tower on one of the least traveled sections of the Long Trail.

General location: Eden Mills
Distance: 7.9-mile lollipop
Hiking time: About 6 hours
Highest point: 3,360 feet
Elevation gain: 2,140 feet
Difficulty: Very strenuous (due to elevation gain)
When to go: Year-round, except during mud season
Canine compatibility: Dog friendly

Trail surface: Packed dirt, mud, rocks
Land status: Public
Nearest amenities: Eden
Trail users: Hikers, snowshoers
Water availability: Brook behind Tillotson Camp
Maps: USGS Eden and Hazen's Notch quads
Special considerations: None
Trail contact: Green Mountain Club, (802) 244-7037, www.greenmountainclub.org

Finding the trailhead: From Route 100 in Eden Mills, bear left on North Road, which becomes Mines Road. Go 5.1 miles to Tillotson Road. Turn left on Tillotson Road (dirt), which narrows and ends at the trailhead parking area. The trailhead is at the back left side (southwest corner) of the parking area.

The Hike

From the trailhead, take the Frank Post Trail (blue blazes) into the ferns and hardwoods. The trail can be wet and muddy at first, climbing gently on its approach toward the mountain.

At 0.6 mile the trail comes to a fork, the junction with the Forester Trail. You will close the loop here on your descent. Bear right, continuing on the Frank Post Trail. The trail immediately crosses a stream and then continues its moderate, steady, uphill stroll. Moose tracks and scat are common sights on the trail.

The route continues southwest, levels off for a bit, and then continues uphill again. The footing is generally smooth. At 1.4 miles it passes a small mud pool. Above the mud pool, waist-high maple saplings encroach on the trail, cooling you as you rustle through their leaves during the summer.

At 1.6 miles the trail becomes scattered with rocks and roots, and the softwoods become more apparent. It rounds a sharp bend to the right and then ascends a couple of switchbacks up a steeper pitch before resuming its generally northwestern course.

A short while later, the path clambers across a 4-foot rock rib with interesting swirls in the rock and a streamlet below it. The way turns steeper and more eroded as you ascend another incline, cross a streamlet, and arrive at Tillotson Camp at 2.0 miles.

Hiker at the foggy summit of Belvidere Mountain by the base of the fire tower. LISA BALLARD

Built by the Green Mountain Club in 1939, Tillotson Camp is a rustic but sturdy cabin that sleeps eight on wood "shelves" (bunks) common to cabins on the Long Trail (LT). It is available on a first-come, first-served basis. There is a nice view to the southeast from the cabin itself, with a more expansive view in the same direction from the base of a rocky outcropping through the trees on the far side of the building. This perfect picnic perch is at the base of what looks like an ancient rockslide, although it was more likely a glacial deposit. A brook draining from some nearby beaver ponds serves as a water source 100 feet north of the cabin.

Proceed behind the cabin to the junction with the LT (white blazes). Turn left on the LT–South, climbing past a jumble of boulders. After crossing a streamlet, the trail winds past the right side of a beaver meadow. The beaver pond is just over the next rise.

The path traverses along the southeastern side of the pond and, a few minutes later, crosses a wet plateau. It descends gently and then bends left (west) out of the mud, still on a gentle descent. Although it climbs briefly in a few spots, the long, gentle descent burns up mileage quickly.

Eventually the trail turns uphill, then eases again as it passes into the boreal forest. It levels off on a high ridge. There are no views here, but you sense the sky to either side through the trees. A few minutes later, the canopy opens overhead, but there

Belvidere Mountain Loop

are still no view as you cross another muddy plateau. Finally, a view to the left (east) appears through some low trees.

The trail dips slightly and then leaves the canopy again, opening along a lawn of ferns, bunchberries, and low scrub firs at 4.4 miles.

At 4.8 miles the trail reaches an offset four-way junction in a grassy clearing. The LT–South bends to the right. The sign reading "Forester Trail and Summit" points to the left, but they are not the same left. The Forester Trail, your route down, is a 90-degree left turn (northeast) about 20 yards before the turn for the tower. Take the short spur to the tower (blue blazes), which bends more gradually to the left (east), opposite the turn for the LT–South.

At 5.0 miles the trail comes to the fire tower. The 50-foot tower is one of only three remaining towers on the LT. The other two are on top of Glastonbury and Stratton Mountains in the southern part of the state. This tower was built in the early 1900s and then rebuilt in the 1990s. From its viewing platform, you can see much of the spine of the Green Mountains, the Cold Hollow Mountains, and several Canadian peaks to the north. On clear days, Mount Washington in New Hampshire sits atop the eastern horizon, 71 miles away.

Even without the fire tower, the summit offers excellent views to the east. You can also see the scars of the former asbestos mine on the eastern side of the mountain, which operated from 1899 through 1993.

Return to the staggered junction with the LT and Forester Trail at 5.2 miles. Turn right onto the LT–North, then turn right again about 20 yards later onto the Forester Trail (unmarked). The Forester Trail descends steadily, and the footing is generally smooth, interrupted mainly by patches of mud and moose scat.

The trail crosses a stream, then an overgrown logging road, and then another stream before coming to the junction with the Frank Post Trail at 7.3 miles, closing the loop. Turn right (east) on the Frank Post Trail, retracing your steps for the last 0.6 mile. Arrive back at the trailhead at 7.9 miles.

Miles and Directions

0.0   Start at the trailhead for the Frank Post Trail.

0.6   Bear right at the junction with the Forester Trail, continuing on the Frank Post Trail.

2.0   TILLOTSON CAMP! Go behind the cabin and turn left on the LT-South.

4.4   Leave the forest canopy.

4.8   Take the second left onto the spur trail to the fire tower.

5.0   FIRE TOWER! Retrace back to the four-way junction with the LT and the Forester Trail. Descend via the Forester Trail.

5.2   Turn right at the junction with the LT, then right again 20 yards later onto the Forester Trail.

7.3   Close the loop at the junction with the Frank Post Trail, continuing downhill toward the trailhead.

7.9   Arrive back at the trailhead.

36 Wheeler Mountain

A fun scramble over open ledges and along a cliff to a nice view of Lake Willoughby and the surrounding mountains.

General location: Barton
Distance: 4.6 miles out and back
Hiking time: About 3 hours
Highest point: 2,371 feet
Elevation gain: 850 feet
Difficulty: Moderate
When to go: Year-round, except during mud season
Canine compatibility: Dog friendly, though there are several difficult ledgy sections and cliff areas.
Trail surface: Packed dirt, rocks, ledgy scrambles

Land status: Public
Trail users: Hikers, snowshoers
Water availability: None
Map: USGS Sutton quad
Special considerations: Crampons or micro-spikes are required if conditions are icy.
Trail contact: Vermont Department of Forests, Parks and Recreation, (802) 751-0136, www .fpr.vermont.gov/willoughby-state-forest; Westmore Association, www.westmoreassociation .org; NorthWoods Stewardship Center, (802) 723-6551, www.northwoodscenter.org

Finding the trailhead: From the junction of US 5 and Route 5A in West Burke, go 8.3 miles north on US 5 toward Barton. Turn right (northeast) on Wheeler Mountain Road (dirt) and go 1.5 miles. The trailhead parking area is on the right (east) side of the road.

The Hike

Wheeler Mountain is definitely in the category of a small hike with a big reward. Though it has a wooded summit, the journey there is largely over open slab and traverses a dramatic cliff. This hike goes over Wheeler's summit and continues to Eagle Point, a rocky perch with a truly incredible view of the Lake Willoughby region.

The trail was completely redone in 2016; the previous parking area (basically just a pullout) and loop hike over private land suffered from overuse and less-than-perfect user behavior. The State of Vermont, local nonprofits, and a landowner collaborated on a plan that resulted in a true parking area and a trail mostly on state land, except for a section through private land that is protected by an easement. A teenage work crew from the NorthWoods Stewardship Center, an organization that maintains and manages several trails in Vermont's Northeast Kingdom, built the new trail. The project is a great example of cooperation among landowners and agencies, and the need to respect trails. Wheeler Mountain is a superb hike to which we would not want to lose access!

From the far corner of the parking area, the Wheeler Mountain Trail (blue blazes) ducks through the woods to Wheeler Mountain Road. It crosses the road and heads over a smooth dirt track through mixed hardwoods. At 0.6 mile the track bends to

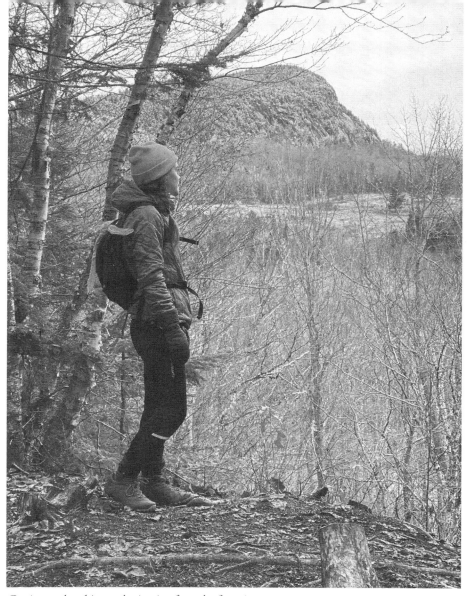

Gazing at the ultimate destination from the first vista. MARK AIKEN

the right, passing through an area surrounded by large boulders. Just past the boulders is a lookout on the right (northeast) side of the trail, affording a view of your destination, Wheeler Mountain, with its exposed granite and sheer cliffs.

At 1.0 mile the trail—still dirt—begins a gentle sidehill ascent. At 1.3 miles it enters a grove of hemlocks and crosses the first of many slabby sections. To the right is a spur to another lookout. Lowell Mountain and its massive wind turbines dominate the view. The turbines are part of the Kingdom Community Wind project that includes twenty-one windmills over a 3.5-mile ridgeline. Built between 2010 and

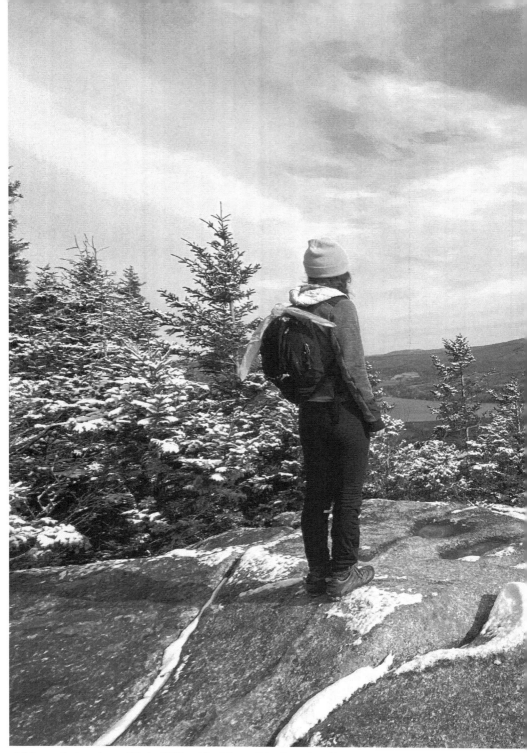
A hiker enjoying views of Lake Willoughby, Mount Pisgah, and Bald Mountain from Eagle Point on Wheeler Mountain. MARK AIKEN

Wheeler Mountain

Eagle Point

Wheeler Mountain

Wheeler Mountain Trail

Wheeler Brook

36 P

Wheeler Mountain Road

Wheeler Pond

2012, the windmills generate 63 megawatts of energy along with much local controversy. Regardless of where one falls in the debate over wind power, the 450-foot-tall windmills are marvels of engineering with their 170-foot-long turbine blades.

At 1.5 miles the trail descends abruptly over switchbacks before breaking out of the forest canopy at 1.7 miles with another view of Lowell Mountain. From here the blue blazes are painted on the ground as you ascend over rocky slab, climbing to a spine and then a cliff edge. At the top of the spine, a dazzling panorama awaits. Bald Mountain with its fire tower, Mount Pisgah, and Mount Hor are directly east. Looking south, Burke Mountain looms behind Lowell Mountain, and, farther away, Mount Mansfield is over your shoulder to the southwest.

The trail follows the cliff line through some low trees, bending northeast. It passes another small rock perch, then enters the woods again until it reaches the wooded summit of the mountain at 2.0 miles. From here it dips steeply and then traverses to Eagle Point at 2.3 miles. This perch is a living room-size lookout over a 500-foot drop. Farms and forest lie below, and there is an expansive view to the east of Lake Willoughby with Mount Pisgah's tall cliffs on the far shore. Bald Mountain is to the north, set back from the lake, and Burke Mountain remains in view to the south.

Locally, Wheeler Mountain is known as a perfect family outing. I would agree that kids will be captivated by the rocky scrambles. Be sure to educate them, however, that the upper reaches of Wheeler are no place for fooling around or wandering close to edges.

Return by the same route.

Miles and Directions

0.0 Start at the far corner of the parking area on the Wheeler Mountain Trail (blue blazes).

0.1 Cross the road you drove in on.

0.6 Bend right through large boulders, passing a lookout on the right side with a view of Wheeler Mountain.

1.3 Enter a hemlock grove. A spur to the right leads to a view of Lowell Mountain.

1.7 Climb a rock spine to the edge of a cliff. Traverse the cliff edge as you climb.

2.0 SUMMIT! Continue over the wooded summit.

2.3 EAGLE POINT! Return by the same route.

4.6 Arrive back at the trailhead.

37 Mount Pisgah via the South Trail

A well-maintained footpath that begins with a long bridge through a sizable beaver pond and then passes a precipitous perch over Lake Willoughby en route to the top of the cliff that forms the eastern wall of Willoughby Gap.

General location: Westmore
Distance: 3.4 miles out and back
Hiking time: About 3 hours
Highest point: 2,751 feet
Elevation gain: 1,450 feet
Difficulty: More challenging
When to go: Year-round, except during mud season
Canine compatibility: Dog friendly, but be aware of precipitous cliff edges.
Trail surface: Packed dirt

Land status: Public
Trail users: Hikers, snowshoers
Water availability: None
Map: USGS Sutton quad
Special considerations: None
Trail contact: Vermont Department of Forests, Parks and Recreation, (802) 751-0136, www .fpr.vermont.gov/willoughby-state-forest; Westmore Association, www.westmoreassociation .org; NorthWoods Stewardship Center, (802) 723-6551, www.northwoodscenter.org

Finding the trailhead: Take Route 5A north from West Burke or south from Westmore. The trailhead is just south of Lake Willoughby on the east side of the road, marked by a sign that says "Willoughby State Forest Trailhead." The best parking is at the trailhead. Additional parking is available across the road at the trailhead for Mount Hor.

The Hike

Mount Pisgah in northern Vermont defines the eastern wall of Willoughby Gap on the eastern side of Lake Willoughby, a landlocked fjord that is both a National Natural Landmark and a designated state natural area. The lake is the centerpiece of 7,300-acre Willoughby State Forest, which was established in 1928. It is sometimes called "the Lucerne of America" for its shape and the way the mountains on either side of it rise so steeply.

Lake Willoughby is a mecca for local divers because its water is extremely clear for a lake, often with over 50 feet visibility, and because it is deep, 312 feet at its deepest point, with an average depth of 123 feet. Some of the biggest lake trout in Vermont, weighing over 30 pounds, have come out of the cold, deep waters of this lake, which is geologically unique to Vermont. It is literally a granite trough that was formed by the glaciers that covered this region during the last ice age.

Mount Pisgah offers some of the more spectacular views of the lake, but it is not a great choice if you are afraid of heights, or, as a fellow hiker once stated, "I'm not scared of heights. I'm scared of edges." One perch in particular, called Pulpit Rock, provides a particularly dizzying view of the lake.

A hiker on Pulpit Rock. LISA BALLARD

The South Trail, which is the oldest trail up the mountain, starts out tamely enough, crossing a sizable beaver pond called Swampy's Pond on a footbridge. The trail bends around the pond through a mixed forest of hemlock, birch, and maple, giving the area an Adirondack feel. It remains relatively flat as it winds past moss-covered boulders that seem to have been thrown at random throughout the woods.

At 0.4 mile the trail turns left and begins climbing steadily. It remains wide, with good footing, and is in excellent condition thanks to a local youth group from Westmore that spends their summers on the trail crew here.

There are numerous glimpses of the lake and Mount Hor, the opposite wall of Willoughby Gap, through the trees as you ascend past rough-hewn handrails. The first clear overlook is slightly farther, over a hedge of low cedars. Watch your step. It is a big drop!

At 0.9 mile Pulpit Rock bulges from the cliff, offering an unobstructed view of the entire lake, the cliffs to the right, Mount Hor across the gap, and a small marina 650 feet below. Use caution at every lookout, but especially this one. Stay low to get close to the edge, and give it a lot of respect. There are no guardrails.

Above Pulpit Rock the trail bends right, away from the cliff area, and flattens out for a short stretch. Just as it begins to climb again, check out the large boulders on the

Kilometer

Mile

N

5A

North Trail

Mount
Pisgah

Pulpit
Rock ▲

Lake
Willoughby

WILLOUGHBY
STATE FOREST

South Trail

▲ Mount
Hor

Swampy's
Pond

37

5A

To West Burke

right, which were actually one boulder until it broke apart. Today, it looks like a huge 3-D puzzle waiting to be put back together.

The trail climbs more moderately as it winds back toward the lake, passing through a birch grove and dipping over a single log bridge. The route becomes rougher and rockier before turning away from the lake again.

At 1.7 miles the trail climbs up a rock slab to open rock amid the scrub trees. The word *Trail*, with an arrow pointing both north and south, is painted in yellow on the rock. The trail beyond, dubbed the "North Trail," continues back to Route 5A on the northern side of Mount Pisgah, 5.5 miles from the South trailhead. While technically not above tree line and not the summit, this open area is close enough and sizable enough for a summit picnic, and offers views to the south toward Burke Mountain, Newark Pond, and even the White Mountains on a clear day. The real summit is a few steps farther, unmarked, in the trees.

Return by the same route.

Miles and Directions

0.0   Start at the trailhead for the South Trail. Cross a beaver pond on a low wooden bridge.

0.4   The trail bends left (north) and begins to climb.

0.9   PULPIT ROCK! Ease your way to the edge for a view of Lake Willoughby, then continue climbing.

1.7   SUMMIT! Return by the same route.

3.4   Arrive back at the trailhead.

38 Bald Mountain (Westmore)

A long approach, then a steady climb to a grassy clearing and a tall fire tower, with commanding views into Quebec and of New Hampshire's White Mountains.

General location: Westmore
Distance: 4.0 miles out and back
Hiking time: About 3.5 hours
Highest point: 3,315 feet
Elevation gain: 1,450 feet
Difficulty: More challenging
When to go: Year-round, except during mud season
Canine compatibility: Dog friendly
Trail surface: Packed dirt
Land status: The summit of Bald Mountain is on state-owned land. The rest of the hike is on private property. The owners live nearby and ask hikers to leave no trace and respect their land.
Trail users: Hikers, snowshoers
Water availability: None
Map: USGS Island Pond quad
Special considerations: None
Trail contact: Vermont Department of Forests, Parks and Recreation, (802) 751-0136, www .fpr.vermont.gov; Westmore Association, www .westmoreassociation.org; NorthWoods Stewardship Center, (802) 723-6551, www.north woodscenter.org

Finding the trailhead: Follow Route 5A along the shore of Lake Willoughby. In Westmore, turn east onto Long Pond Road. The trailhead and a small parking area are on the left, 0.1 mile after the boat access on Long Pond. Please do not block the gate.

The Hike

Bald Mountain in Westmore is not only the tallest Bald Mountain in Vermont, it is also the tallest peak in the Lake Willoughby area. Don't be fooled by the name. Like the other Bald Mountains in Vermont, this one does not have a bald summit, but it does have other redeeming features. This Bald Mountain is the only one with an elevation above 3,000 feet. It was once clear as a result of a forest fire, but gradually the flora returned. Today, the summit is a broad, grassy area with an old shelter on one side and an outstanding fire tower in the middle.

There are two approaches to the summit. The North Trail departs from Mad Brook Road. The South Trail departs from Long Pond Road and is described here because it is easier to find and has better parking.

The trail begins on an old dirt logging road that is now as much grass as gravel. At the first fork, bear right. A sign on a tree says "Trail," with an arrow underneath it pointing to the right. A short distance later, in a small clearing, the trail forks again. Bear right again at the end of the clearing. A few minutes later, the trail bends left into the woods and flattens, becoming more footpath than road, and blue blazes appear on the trees. The path traverses slightly downhill through a deciduous forest with a full canopy overhead. The many maple trees make this a colorful area during fall foliage.

The fire tower on top of Bald Mountain. LISA BALLARD

Bald Mountain (Westmore)

0 Kilometer 0.5
0 Mile 0.5

N

GOODWIN MOUNTAIN

Mad Brook Trail (North Trail)

Long Pond–Bald Mtn Trail (South Trail)

Bald Mountain

Rock Overhang

Mill Brook

39 P

To Route 5A and Westmore

Long Pond

Long Pond Road

Haystack Mountain

To Route 5A and West Burke

At 1.0 mile the trail crosses a streamlet, the first of several stream crossings, none of which are reliable.

After three consecutive stream crossings, the route starts to climb gently. After another small stream crossing and a series of log steps, the trail meanders through the woods on its long approach to the mountain. About ten minutes later, the uphill climb starts in earnest, passing over a split-log bridge and then through a couple of short switchbacks before taking a more direct line up the slope. The footing remains relatively good, though more roots crisscross the trail.

At 1.7 miles the trail bends left, passing an impressive rock overhang, 4 feet high and about 15 feet long, as if a giant wedge had been taken out of the mountainside. A root from a birch tree grows down and the trunk of another tree grows up, like two pillars in front of the shallow cave.

The trail climbs more sharply above the overhang, through a spruce grove, immediately passing an odd hole on the right. It crosses a tangle of roots and slab before reaching a short but hefty log bridge. The bridge crosses a narrow rock chasm, only a foot across and 6 feet deep.

From here it is a short, steady climb to the summit. The fire tower has been restored by volunteers from the North Woods Stewardship Center, the Northeast section of the Green Mountain Club, and the Westmore Association. The view from the tower is impressive on a clear day. To the south, Bald Hill Pond (close) and Newark Pond (farther) point toward Burke Mountain. The end of Lake Willoughby is visible to the west over the right shoulder of Haystack Mountain. Beyond Haystack, you can see Mount Pisgah and then Mount Hor on either side of Lake Willoughby. The cliffs beyond belong to Wheeler Mountain. Several peaks in Quebec lie to the north across Lake Memphremagog, and the towering Presidential Range in New Hampshire lies on the southeastern horizon.

Return by the same route.

Miles and Directions

0.0   Start on the South Trail, also called the Long Pond–Bald Mountain Trail, near Long Pond.

1.0   Cross the first of several streamlets.

1.7   Pass a small cave formed by a large rock overhang embedded in the side of the mountain.

2.0   SUMMIT! Return by the same route.

4.0   Arrive back at the trailhead.

39 Bluff Mountain Loop

An adrenaline-filled ascent to an overlook of Island Pond.

General location: Island Pond
Distance: 3.1-mile lollipop
Hiking time: About 2.5 hours
Highest point: 2,380 feet
Elevation gain: 1,080 feet
Difficulty: More challenging (due to one vertical, rocky section, which can be bypassed)
When to go: Year-round, except during mud season
Canine compatibility: Most dogs will be challenged on the ledgy, ladder-assisted section of the Lookout Trail. There are alternative routes.

Trail surface: Packed dirt, rocks, ledges with metal ladder rungs and handholds
Land status: Public
Trail users: Hikers, snowshoers
Water availability: None
Map: USGS Spectacle Pond quad
Special considerations: None
Trail contact: Green Mountain Club, (802) 244-7037, www.greenmountainclub.org; Vermont Department of Forests, Parks and Recreation, (802) 886-2215, www.vtstateparks.com

Finding the trailhead: From the junction of Routes 105 and 114 in Island Pond, go east on Route 105 for 0.1 mile. After the bridge, take a left on South Street. Go 0.2 mile and turn right on Mountain Street. Follow Mountain Street for 0.6 mile to the trailhead parking area on the left (north) side of the road.

The Hike

For proof that good things come from cooperation and teamwork, look no further than the Kingdom Heritage Trail. In 1998, ownership of 132,000 acres of wild forestland in Vermont's Northeast Kingdom transferred from the Champion International paper company and was divvied among the State of Vermont, the US Fish and Wildlife Service, and private owners. An easement ensures public access to a trail corridor through this wild and beautiful area. After twenty years of planning and trail construction, state and federal agencies, the Green Mountain Club and other organizations, and many volunteers created the Kingdom Heritage Trail network—over 20 miles of footpaths through one of Vermont's least populated regions. Opened in 2019, it is the newest backcountry trail network in Vermont. The route to the summit of Bluff Mountain is part of this network.

From the trailhead, the Bluff Mountain Community Trail (blue blazes) passes a trail register in a human-planted stand of red pines and begins to climb through a mixed hardwood forest. At 0.7 mile turn left at Lookout Junction onto the yellow-blazed Lookout Trail. You'll close your loop here on the return trip, unless you want to avoid a technical, ladder-assisted section ahead. There are two easy options for bypassing the more advanced section; staying on the Bluff Trail here is the first.

Island Pond from the lookout near the summit of Bluff Mountain. MARK AIKEN

The Lookout Trail descends for a third of a mile through new-growth maples and birches before coming to Basin Junction at 1.0 mile. This is the second and last chance to avoid the ladder-assisted challenge ahead, by turning right on the Basin Link Trail, which connects back to the Bluff Mountain Trail. Courageous adrenaline seekers (and the most sure-footed canines) can continue straight on the Lookout Trail, which turns steeply uphill. For the next third of a mile, trail builders have installed metal rungs and handrails to assist ascending hikers. Don't forget to look over your shoulder as you climb. The views through the trees of Island Pond won't disappoint you.

At 1.4 miles, at the top of the aided ascent, you come to a lookout and the best view on Bluff Mountain. The summit a short distance ahead does not boast unobstructed views. If you bypassed the difficult ascent, be sure to visit this perch for the view. Bluff Mountain rises adjacent to the village of Island Pond, and the hamlet is directly below you. Look south to see the pond, and the island for which it is named, in front of Starr and Seneca Mountains. Burke Mountain looms in the distance. This is a great place for lunch or a snack.

Beyond the lookout, the trail ascends gently over packed dirt and roots, through hemlocks and twisted, peeling birches, to the junction with the Bluff Mountain Trail at 1.6 miles. The summit is a few steps to the left on the Bluff Mountain Trail. For

Hiking aids on the steep ascent on the Lookout Trail. MARK AIKEN

Bluff Mountain Loop

those looking for a longer hike, the Bluff Mountain Trail runs for miles along a ridgeline through a rugged forest. Views at sporadic clearings along the trail capture the vastness and remoteness of Vermont's Northeast Kingdom, the state's least populated corner. Don't expect a cell signal on this hike or in many of the villages below.

From the summit of Bluff Mountain, return on the Bluff Mountain Trail, which descends gradually over packed earth and puncheons before a junction with Basin Link at 2.1 miles. Stay left on the Bluff Mountain Trail, descending a set of stone stairs, then follow the trail to the junction with the Lookout Trail at 2.4 miles. Retrace from here back to the trailhead at 3.1 miles.

Miles and Directions

0.0   Start at the trailhead for the Bluff Mountain Trail.

0.7   Turn left on the Lookout Trail (or stay straight on the Bluff Mountain Trail to avoid the technical section ahead).

1.0   Stay straight on the Lookout Trail (or turn right on Basin Link to avoid the technical section ahead).

1.4   VIEW! From the lookout on the shoulder of Bluff Mountain, descend gently to the junction with the Bluff Mountain Trail, then turn left to reach the summit.

1.6   SUMMIT! Descend straight ahead, on the Bluff Mountain Trail.

2.1   Remain on the Bluff Mountain Trail (left fork) at the junction with the Basin Link Trail.

2.4   Continue straight on the Bluff Mountain Trail at the junction with the Lookout Trail.

3.1   Arrive back at the trailhead.

40 Jay Peak

Short hike on the Long Trail to the open rocky top of Vermont's northernmost ski area, with stellar views into southern Quebec.

General location: Jay
Distance: 3.4 miles out and back with a loop
Hiking time: About 3.5 hours
Highest point: 3,861 feet
Elevation gain: 1,680 feet
Difficulty: More challenging (due to elevation gain)
When to go: Year-round, except for mud season
Canine compatibility: Dog friendly
Trail surface: Packed dirt, rocks, slab

Land status: Public
Trail users: Hikers, snowshoers, skiers
Water availability: Spring at Jay Camp
Map: USGS Jay Peak quad
Special considerations: None
Trail contact: Vermont Department of Forests, Parks and Recreation, (802) 751-0110, www.fpr.vermont.gov/jay-state-forest-big-jayblack-falls-tracts; Green Mountain Club, (802) 244-7037, www.greenmountainclub.org

Finding the trailhead: Take Route 242 southeast of the Jay Peak ski area to a height of land known as Jay Pass. Watch for the turnout on the left (east) side of the road, which is the trailhead parking area. The trailhead is on the opposite side of the road. The Long Trail (LT) crosses the road at this point. There is no obvious sign, though you can see a small shelter on the right at the edge of the woods.

The Hike

Enter the woods on the LT–North (white blazes), immediately passing the Atlas Valley Shelter, a four-person lean-to that was built in 1967 from wood supplied by the Atlas timber company. It was not intended for overnight use, but it works in a pinch. The main trail starts out as much stream as footpath after a heavy rain, but the footing is easy. It soon begins to climb, getting increasingly steeper and becoming rockier and more well-worn.

At 0.1 mile the LT comes to a junction with Jay Loop (blue blazes) to Jay Camp. Turn left (southwest) onto Jay Loop. Jay Camp is a cabin maintained by the Green Mountain Club, and a much better choice than the tiny Atlas Valley Shelter for those wishing to spend the night.

The path to Jay Camp is flat and wet. It reaches the cabin at 0.3 mile. Constructed in 1958, it sleeps eight to twelve people and has a reliable spring about 50 feet away.

Jay Loop swings back toward the LT to the right of the cabin, rejoining it at 0.5 mile. Turn left on the LT–North, continuing toward the summit. From here the trail goes up, curves, goes up more, and then curves again in a generally northwestern direction. It does not have switchbacks per se, just arcing turns.

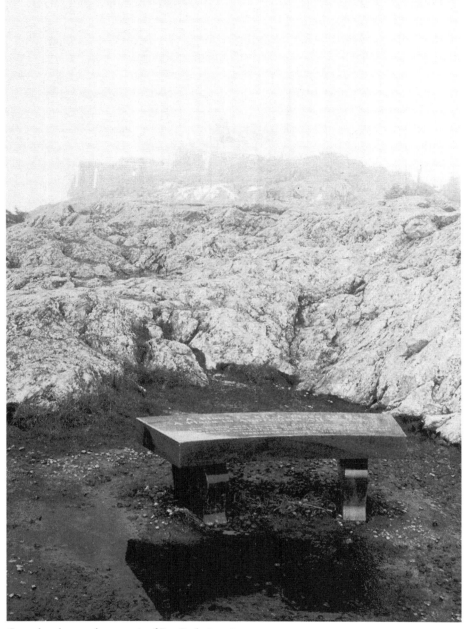

Stone bench near the summit of Jay Peak. LISA BALLARD

At 0.6 mile the softwoods start to intrude. The trail eases, winding through a berry patch. Watch the prickers along the side of the trail. The grade remains easy as the berries give way to ferns, and evergreens take over.

At 0.9 mile there is a break in the trees to the left, with a nice view of the neighboring peaks to the north and into Canada. Around the next bend, the path

0   Kilometer   0.5

0   Mile   0.5

N

JAY STATE FOREST

To Jay

Tram
Terminal

Jay Peak

Long Trail

242

Atlas
Valley
Shelter

Jay Loop

Jay Camp

40   P

Long Trail

To Montgomery

gets steeper again, crossing short sections of slab and climbing up a number of stone steps. Nothing is extreme to this point; however, the upper part of the climb is more challenging.

Soon the spruce trees close in on the sides of the trail, which begins a longer, more sustained climb than any point so far, crossing sections of rough slab and rock. The trail makes a sharp left just below a ski trail, noticeable mainly because of the snowmaking pipes that run along the ground above the turn. After that, the slabs lengthen and can be slippery.

At 1.6 miles the LT meets Jay Peak Resort's Vermonter ski trail. Cross the ski trail, continuing on the LT, which heads up an open ridge parallel to the ski trail. The LT is more interesting. It goes over a rocky hump and then climbs steadily toward the summit cone, passing a polished stone bench just below the tram terminal at 1.8 miles.

Many hikers stop at the polished bench, away from the tourists around the tram. The bench was placed there in 2001 in memory of Dick Meunier, an employee of Jay Peak for thirty-eight years. It is inscribed with the words "A place to sit, a place to be, a place to appreciate all that we see." And there is certainly a lot to see. To the south, you can look down the spine of the Green Mountains as far as Camel's Hump. The White Mountains and the Adirondacks are visible to the southeast and southwest, respectively. To the north lies the Sutton Range in Quebec. The large lake to the northeast is Lake Memphremagog, which straddles the Canadian border.

Return by the same route, remaining on the LT–South the entire way, which is about 0.2 mile shorter than hiking around Jay Loop again. Arrive back at the trailhead at 3.4 miles.

Miles and Directions

0.0 Start on the LT-North where it crosses Route 242.

0.1 Turn left at the lower junction of the LT and Jay Loop toward Jay Camp.

0.3 JAY CAMP! Continue on Jay Loop back to the LT.

0.5 Turn left (north) at the upper junction of the LT and Jay Loop, continuing toward the summit.

0.6 Pass through a berry patch.

0.9 First view to the north through a break in the trees.

1.6 Cross a ski trail and head up a rocky ledge onto the summit ridge.

1.8 SUMMIT! Return the entire way along the LT-South.

3.4 Arrive back at the trailhead.

Appendix A: For More Information

In case of emergency, call 911.

Trail Maintenance Organizations

Appalachian Trail Conservancy
(304) 535-6331
www.appalachiantrail.org

Green Mountain Club Headquarters and Marvin B. Gameroff Hiker Information Center
(802) 244-7037
www.greenmountainclub.org

Moosalamoo Association
(802) 989-6980
www.moosalamoo.org

NorthWoods Stewardship Center
(802) 723-6551, ext. 301
www.northwoodscenter.org

Westmore Association
westmoreassociation.org

Government Agencies

Green Mountain National Forest
www.fs.fed.us/r9/gmfl
Manchester Ranger District
(802) 362-2307
Rochester/Middlebury Ranger District
(802) 767-4261
Rutland Supervisor's Office
(802) 747-6700

Vermont Department of Forests, Parks and Recreation
(802) 241-3655
www.vtstateparks.com or www.state.vt.us/anr

Appendix B: Further Reading and Resources

Guidebooks

Best Hikes with Dogs: New Hampshire & Vermont by Lisa Densmore (The Mountaineers Books, 2005).
Day Hiker's Guide to Vermont, 6th edition (Green Mountain Club, 2011).
Field Guide to North American Trees—Eastern Region by National Audubon Society (Alfred A. Knopf, 2001).
Guide to Vermont's Day Hikes by Jared Grange (Huntington Graphics, 2006).
Long Trail Guide, centennial (28th) edition (Green Mountain Club, 2017).
Nature Guide to Vermont's Long Trail by Lexi Shear (Green Mountain Club, 2008).
Snowshoeing in Vermont: A Guide to the Best Winter Hikes (Green Mountain Club, 2005).
Wildflowers of Vermont, 2nd edition, by Kate Carter (Cotton Brook Publications, 2005).

Maps

Vermont Atlas & Gazetteer (DeLorme)
Vermont's Long Trail, 5th edition (Green Mountain Club)
Westmore Trail Association Map (Westmore Trail Association)

Websites

www.hikesafe.com
www.topozone.com
www.trailfinder.info

Hike Index

THE TEN ESSENTIALS OF HIKING

American Hiking Society

American Hiking Society recommends you pack the "Ten Essentials" every time you head out for a hike. Whether you plan to be gone for a couple of hours or several months, make sure to pack these items. Become familiar with these items and know how to use them.

1. Appropriate Footwear
Happy feet make for pleasant hiking. Think about traction, support, and protection when selecting well-fitting shoes or boots.

2. Navigation
While phones and GPS units are handy, they aren't always reliable in the backcountry; consider carrying a paper map and compass as a backup and know how to use them.

3. Water (and a way to purify it)
As a guideline, plan for half a liter of water per hour in moderate temperatures/terrain. Carry enough water for your trip and know where and how to treat water while you're out on the trail.

4. Food
Pack calorie-dense foods to help fuel your hike, and carry an extra portion in case you are out longer than expected.

5. Rain Gear & Dry-Fast Layers
The weatherman is not always right. Dress in layers to adjust to changing weather and activity levels. Wear moisture-wicking clothes and carry a warm hat.

6. Safety Items (light, fire, and a whistle)
Have means to start an emergency fire, signal for help, and see the trail and your map in the dark.

7. First Aid Kit
Supplies to treat illness or injury are only as helpful as your knowledge of how to use them. Take a class to gain the skills needed to administer first aid and CPR.

8. Knife or Multi-Tool
With countless uses, a multi-tool can help with gear repair and first aid.

9. Sun Protection
Sunscreen, sunglasses, and sun-protective clothing should be used in every season regardless of temperature or cloud cover.

10. Shelter
Protection from the elements in the event you are injured or stranded is necessary. A lightweight, inexpensive space blanket is a great option.

Find other helpful resources at AmericanHiking.org/hiking-resources

PROTECT THE PLACES YOU LOVE TO HIKE.
Become a member today and take $5 off an annual membership using the code **Falcon5**.

AmericanHiking.org/join

American Hiking Society is the only national nonprofit organization dedicated to empowering all to enjoy, share, and preserve the hiking experience.

American
Hiking
Society